ISLAND PUBBING II

A Guide to Pubs on Vancouver Island
and the Gulf Islands

Robert Moyes

Orca Book Publishers

First Edition

Canadian Cataloguing in Publication Data

Moyes, Robert; 1953—
  Island pubbing II

ISBN 0-920501-60-5

1. Hotels, taverns, etc.—British Columbia—Vancouver Island—Guide-books.
2. Hotels, taverns, etc.—British Columbia—Gulf Islands—Guide-books.
3. Vancouver Island (B.C.)—Description and travel—Guide-books. 4. Gulf Islands (B.C.)—Description and travel—Guide-books. I. Title
TX950.59.C3M69 1991   647.95711'2   C91-091112-6

Cover design: Susan Fergusson
Printing and binding: Hignell Printing Ltd.

Printed and bound in Canada

Orca Book Publishers
P.O. Box 5626, Station B
Victoria, B.C., V8R 6S4
Canada

With love to
The True Companion

Acknowledgements

This book would have been a much less pleasant task without the help of several friends, who acted as my "designated drinkers" on the longer up-Island explorations or otherwise provided encouragement and technical expertise. Many thanks to: Lynne Bain, Jon Barss, Chris Gower, Lawrence McLagan, Tom Niemann and Randy Smith.

Table of Contents

A Toast to Sensible Drinking

When this book was first printed in 1984, it was appropriate for the introduction to celebrate how the "beer barns" of the 1970s were gradually being supplanted by the friendlier, saner alternative offered by neighbourhood pubs. But what were originally novelties that attracted faraway business have since become the norm, and many residents who were initially sceptical—or downright hostile—about the prospect of having a "noisy tavern" in their backyard have come around to the notion of a civilized and social style of drinking that has been popular in Britain for centuries. Today, Vancouver Island has dozens and dozens of neighbourhood pubs, and these havens of good food, good beer and good times have become so common that they are now truly *neighbourhood* places. The bartenders at establishments such as Christie's, the George and Dragon, Maude Hunter's and the Oxford Arms know most of their clientele . . . many of whom walk to their "local" for a tasty lunch or a few pints of beer and a game of darts to pass a pleasant evening.

Beer drinkers on this Island are particularly lucky. Aside from the ever-expanding number of cosy and attractive drinking spots—where restaurant-quality food and wide-ranging leisure and entertainment options are increasingly the norm—this area has been developing its own special beers. There are four brewpubs (Spinnakers, Swans and the Prairie Inn in the Victoria area, and The Leeward in Comox) that supply a wide range of ales and lagers to appease Island thirsts.

But undoubtedly our biggest thirst quencher is the Vancouver Island Brewing Company, incorporated in Central Saanich in 1984. Although they have always made a good beer, there is no arguing that their current product list is nothing short of outstanding. Currently, their lineup of unpasteurized, all-natural beers includes Vancouver Island

Premium Lager, Piper's Ale, and their signature Bavarian dark lager, Hermann's. More than 150 pubs and restaurants now carry their draught. And their recent move into bottled beer has resulted in bigger sales than expected—look for a 12-pack soon! Yearly output for this splendid brewery tops 1,500,000 litres.

Vernon's Okanagan Spring Brewery—whose fine output includes St. Patrick Stout, Pale Ale and cider—is also a popular choice at the taps. These days, it's rare to walk into a pub that doesn't carry one or more of the tasty brews made by Vancouver Island Brewing or Okanagan Spring. All of these beverages make a refreshing change from the mass-produced beers that, for too long, were the only options.

And the real connoisseurs have been taking advantage of the recently relaxed laws on import draught: the Sticky Wicket and Fogg n' Suds are just two of the places where a gourmet selection of import brews from Britain, Germany and elsewhere is always available.

As our local breweries and brewpubs expand their skills and diversify their product, they are matched by a growing group of tankard hoisters whose passion for the potable is an equal mixture of scholarship, consumer advocacy and a keen interest in the social ramifications of whistle wetting. The British-born CAMRA—The Campaign for Real Ale—has become increasingly active around the world, and is represented in Victoria by a particularly vigorous chapter. Monthly meetings, a lively newsletter, regular special events and a keen commitment to improving their appreciation of the subtleties of man's oldest beverage are the hallmarks of this group. (For information, call 595-7728.)

But even though the proliferation of neighbourhood pubs signals an improvement in our collective drinking habits, it is always appropriate to repeat the message that drinking drivers are a leading cause of death and destruction on B.C.'s roads and highways. Although *Island Pubbing* is an invitation to sample the various delights of pubs scattered all about Vancouver Island, we encourage you to take your pleasures prudently. If some determined partying is planned, then please consider yet another imported drinking custom: arrange for a designated driver or some other safe form of transport.

So much for the sermon. Vancouver Island has a genuine wealth of fine pubs, and lager lovers can now hoist their glasses in log cabins or Tudor palaces, in modern marine pubs or historic roadhouses with a hundred-year tradition of leaving no thirst unslaked.

There are few places in the world where a one-hundred-minute drive could take you from a brew pub-cum-art gallery such as Swans to the unique charms of the Dinghy Dock, a floating pub off Nanaimo's Protection Island that is only accessible by boat or ferry.

And things just keep getting better. Although Hornby Island's The Latch burned down, it is expected to be rebuilt by the summer of 1991. A combination marine-brewpub is being planned along the waterfront in the Capital Iron area, while scenic Sooke Harbour will be the location of the Manuel Quimper Marine Pub by 1992.

In just fifteen years, neighbourhood pubs have gone from novelty status to being the preferred way to savour a beer or a fine meal. For anyone who enjoys a civilized sip and the pleasures of good company, the only thing to say is: Cheers!

The Art of Brewing Beer

Although we can't say for sure where beer was first made, current evidence suggests that brewing was done in Babylon at least 10,000 years ago. We do know that beer was made from malted grain in Mesopotamia in 7000 B.C.; and although the ubiquitous foaming beverage currently has secular associations with football games and dart championships, it once played an important religious role in the Egypt of the pharaohs. Centuries later the Romans displayed their typically efficient style by improving the science of beer-making, incidentally spreading the good news throughout France, Spain and England as they clumped about the known world on a real estate-gathering spree.

Latterly, we have looked to England and Germany as our brew-making role models, and although beer has been made in these countries for a thousand years and more, it's only in the last century—basically since the use of yeast as a fermenting agent was perfected—that brewmasters have been creating beer that would be truly recognizable to our palates.

Brewing is both an art and science, and it comprises three main stages: mashing, boiling and fermentation. Beer is derived from "malted" barley — grain that has been kept moist till it sprouts — then roasted dry in the oven. (Darker beers are produced by roasting the barley more.) The mashing process begins when the malted barley is ground up, then mixed with water to a porridge-like consistency and heated to about 150 degrees F. As the barley cooks, the enzymes developed during the malting process convert grain starches into fermentable sugars. By the end of the mashing phase, the liquefied barley is referred to as "wort."

The wort is now boiled for approximately two hours. It is

during this phase that the hops are added—thus presenting the brewmaster with the first real chance to individualize his product. Hops, which impart to beer its characteristically sharp and attractively tangy taste, come in many varieties. Depending on the amount and type of hops used, and even at what time during the boiling process the hops are added, a brewer can radically affect the taste of his current batch. Immediately following the boiling phase, the bittersweet wort is promptly filtered to remove the hops, and is then rapidly cooled.

When the wort is sufficiently cool, the yeast is added to begin the process of fermentation. Yeast is a primitive plant that feeds on the sugar in beer, giving off alcohol and carbon dioxide in the process. The yeast has such a profound influence on the type and nature of the resulting beer that many brewmasters develop their own unique strains of yeast, the secrets of which are then guarded with police-state rigour. (This fermenting precision would have amazed the beermakers during medieval times: those brewers had to rely on air-borne yeast particles to spark the fermentation process—an inaccurate business, to say the least!)

It is at this fermentation stage that a critical choice is made: are we brewing lager or ale? Lagers—smoother-tasting beers of Germanic origin—are made at cool temperatures and stored for up to a half-year at near-freezing temperatures. Lagers are made with a "bottom-fermenting" yeast that settles on the bottom after the lengthy fermentation process is over. The carbon dioxide that is given off during fermentation is retrieved and stored, only to be reinjected towards the end of the lagering process.

British-born ales, characterized by stronger flavour and a richer texture, are "top-fermented," meaning that the yeast floats to the top after it has done its work. Ale fermentation is done at a higher temperature, for a period of five to seven days. Unlike lagers, ales display lower carbonation and do not require a lengthy storage period to "condition" the beer.

The final steps, at least in terms of larger commercial brewing, include filtration and pasteurization (a necessary evil that does make beer more stable, but also compromises the taste). Finally, the beer is bottled or canned and shipped off to market.

This brief overview of the brewing process isn't really complete without some recent history. After Prohibition, North

American manufacturers seeking a national market opted for lighter, blander beer. To achieve this they cut way back on the malt, using as much as forty percent corn or rice. This ongoing dilution has sapped flavour and created a weaker body in virtually all the big-label beers that you buy at the liquor store. And when you further consider all the preservatives and the artificial "heading" agents that get dumped into the vats these days, then you have most of the reasons why the "real ale" movement has been catching on of late.

Started in England in the 1970s, the Campaign For Real Ale has become a near-religious cause for thousands of beer lovers who insist that their steins should be overflowing with nothing but pure, wholesome, old-fashioned brew. And they've got a good argument! Anyone who lives near a brewpub (or whose "local" stocks the unpasteurized and all-natural beers manufactured by the Vancouver Island Brewing Company or Okanagan Spring Brewery) has the option to sample beer exactly as it was meant to be consumed, with absolutely no chemicals or other concessions made to the large-scale manufacturing and distribution process. Cheers!

The Different Types of Beer

As noted above, the two basic types of beer are ale and lager. The top-fermented ales have stronger flavours, a more pronounced texture, and are darker in colour. In contrast, the bottom-fermented lagers, which derive their name from the German word "lagern" ("storing"), are typically crisp, light and subtle. But within these two categories are a wide range of beer types. As follows:

Ale
Pale Ale, also known as India Pale Ale, is highly hopped, giving it a light and tangy flavour. (Pale Ale was originally brewed in nineteenth-century Britain, and shipped to the troops supporting

the British Raj in India.) This straw- or amber-coloured beer is very popular in England.

Bitter is a distinctive English beer, full-bodied and malty, that is heavily hopped. Bitter is usually made with premium barley, and is considered one of the highest examples of the brewer's art. In Canada, bitter is the beer typically associated with the "real ale" movement.

Mild Ale can vary widely according to area, but is typically less strong than a bitter; it's darker in colour, and moderate use of hops results in a slightly sweeter taste.

Brown Ale is similar to mild ale, but is usually heavier and stronger, being made from darker or even roasted barley malt (Newcastle Brown is a famous example).

Porter was made originally in the early 1700s, and became popular the following century. Although still widely available in Ireland, Porter is a rare catch at the taps elsewhere. It is halfway between an ale and a stout, and even its fans allow that it is something of an acquired taste.

Stout is a velvety, quite alcoholic brew peculiar to Britain. Distinguished by its near-black colour and lushly creamy head, stout is made from heavily roasted barley. The characteristically sharp taste results from the liberal use of hops. The most famous example is Ireland's Guinness extra stout, which is shipped worldwide to its numerous disciples.

Old Ale isn't as heavy or as dark as most brown ales, but it is usually a well-matured beverage and has a high alcohol content.

Lager

Light Lager is brewed from pale malted barley, and has a softer, dry taste. Beck's, Heineken and Budweiser are examples of this lager style (and dieters take note: the "light" refers to colour, not calories).

Pilsner, assuredly the most celebrated type of beer throughout the world, is a special light lager that is brewed exclusively with Saaz hops (most Canadian beer is cast in the Pilsner mould). Czechoslovakia's Pilsener Urquell is the classic example of this beer, which is characterized by a golden colour and a refreshing, briskly hoppy flavour.

Dark Lager is made from roasted malted barley and features a smooth and sweet taste. Heineken Dark is a famous international example, although it's hard to beat Hermann's, that lovable local conjured up by the Vancouver Island Brewing Company.

Bock is a strong, golden-coloured beer that Germans traditionally associate with spring. These heavy brews have a characteristic sweet malt taste and are best served lightly chilled.

Kriek beers are made from cherries. Conditioned in the bottle and not filtered, krieks are of interest to beer aficionados.

Steam Beer

And let's not forget unique steam beer, the only beer style indigenous to North America. It originated in nineteenth-century San Francisco, where the refrigeration necessary to produce the in-demand lager beers was not to be found. Resourceful brewmasters compromised on a hybrid, using a lager yeast at the warmer temperatures appropriate to the ale process. The result was a feisty, strongly hopped beverage that was more ale than lager. Steam beer was carbonated (an unusual procedure for draught beers of the day), and its name presumably derived from the loud hissing sound that emanated from a newly tapped keg. Today, San Francisco's Anchor Brewery is the only facility making this intriguing drink.

Victoria and Area

~

1 — Spinnakers Brew Pub
2 — Swans
3 — The Garrick's Head
4 — The Sticky Wicket
5 — Fogg n' Suds
6 — Oxford Arms Pub
7 — Christie's Carriage House
8 — The George and Dragon
9 — The Snug
10 — The Barley Mow Pub
11 — The Monkey Tree Pub
12 — Maude Hunter's Pub
13 — The Bird of Paradise

14 — The Prairie Inn
15 — The Brig Marine Pub
16 — The Rumrunner
17 — Blue Peter Pub
18 — The Stonehouse Pub
19 — Port-of-Call
20 — The Four Mile Roadhouse
21 — Six-Mile House
22 — Country Rose Pub
23 — Seventeen-Mile House
24 — The Loghouse Pub
25 — Ma Miller's

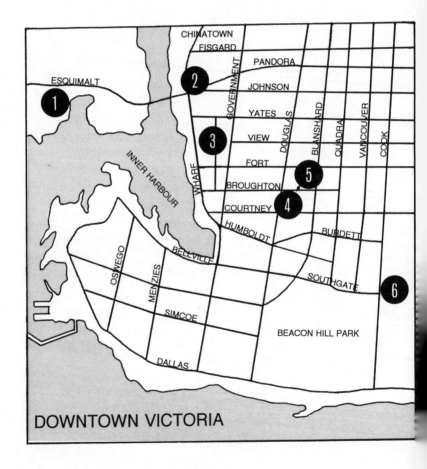

DOWNTOWN VICTORIA

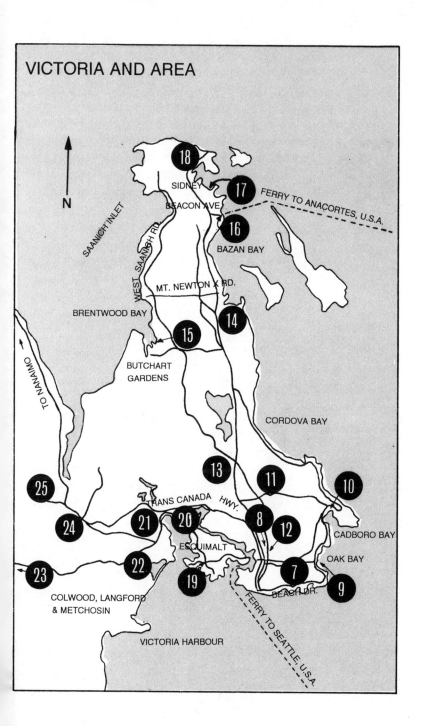

VICTORIA AND AREA

N

SIDNEY

BEACON AVE.

FERRY TO ANACORTES, U.S.A.

SAANICH INLET

WEST SAANICH RD.

BAZAN BAY

MT. NEWTON X RD.

BRENTWOOD BAY

BUTCHART
GARDENS

TO NANAIMO

CORDOVA BAY

TRANS CANADA   HWY.

ESQUIMALT

CADBORO BAY

OAK BAY

BEACH DR.

COLWOOD, LANGFORD
& METCHOSIN

FERRY TO SEATTLE, U.S.A.

VICTORIA HARBOUR

11

Spinnakers Brew Pub

308 Catherine Street, Victoria
Telephone: 384-6613

Hours: 11:00 a.m. - 11:00 p.m., daily

The Navigator: From downtown Victoria, take the Johnson Street Bridge to Esquimalt Road. Turn left at the second set of lights onto Catherine Street. Pub is where the road right-angles towards the Songhees.

Perched at the edge of tiny Lime Bay and overlooking Victoria's Inner Harbour is **Spinnakers Brew Pub**, a virtual shrine to this area's many beer lovers. Canada's first in-house brewpub, Spinnakers uses a "full mash" process that guarantees the highest possible expression of the brewer's art. The shiny vats that you see as you walk up the stairs produce about 40,000 gallons of beer a year, ranging from the straw-coloured Spinnakers Ale to the velvety black Oatmeal Stout. Happily defying Canadian custom, brewmaster Jake Thomas harkens back to the English way of brewing and presenting: the ales are served at slightly warmer temperatures (in order to more fully display their flavour and character), and all the brews are dispensed via authentic porcelain and brass "beer engines" that draw directly from storage vessels in the cellar. Typically, there are eight house brews on tap at any one time (from a roster of about thirty-five), with seasonal specialties and new additions regularly available. And do consider trying the copper-coloured Mitchell's Extra-Special Bitter—in his latest edition of *The World Guide to Beer*, brew guru Michael Jackson rated this as one of the best beers to be had in all of North America.

The recently expanded Spinnakers consists of a main room downstairs, recently licensed as a restaurant, and the new upstairs "taproom," where the original neighbourhood pub licence is now in effect. A cosily handsome establishment, with post and beam construction, brass lamps, lots of plant life and plush oriental carpets, Spinnakers offers superb harbour views of the nearby boating traffic. A spectacular backdrop comes courtesy of the snow-peaked Olympic Mountains. Summertime is heaven out on the patio: you may see

Canada Geese strutting around the nearby posh Songhees condo development, or possibly a lone great blue heron patiently stalking his lunch in the shallows of Lime Bay. Come winter, though, you'll probably want to grab a table near the fire and admire the glowing silhouette of the Parliament Buildings across the way.

The food at Spinnakers is almost as big a draw as its beers: the oysters Rockefeller are superb, while the red snapper Florentine may be the real star of the menu. The finger foods—from hefty french fries to deep-fried zucchini sticks—are great, and the dessert crowd always salutes the deservedly legendary apple pie. Then there's the *entertainment* menu: from old-timey folk jams to fleet-fingered pianists striding through a medley of jazz standards, there's typically something to set your toes a-tappin' whilst savouring the more tangible pleasures here.

With all these qualities, it shouldn't be surprising that this exemplary neighbourhood pub attracts a diverse crowd: Songhees retirees, downtown professionals, university students and people thirsty from a stroll along the West Bay walkway are just some of the types attracted to this special bar that treats beer with all the respect it deserves.

So set your course for Spinnakers, where "they pull a good pint!"

Beer Trivia

Canada's first brewpub was at the Troller Pub in Horseshoe Bay, opened in 1982. (Then-owner John Mitchell went on to open Spinnakers in 1984.)

Pub Philosopher

*"Half of mankind is done in
By alcohol and nicotine
Yet the rest, enjoying neither,
Does not live much longer either."*

— Austrian graffiti

Swans

506 Pandora Street, Victoria
Telephone: 361-3310

Hours: 11:30 - 2:00, Monday - Saturday; 11:30 - midnight, Sunday

The Navigator: Located at the corner of Pandora Avenue and Store Street, just across from Market Square.

There's no doubt that **Swans** should be at or near the top of any beer lover's short list of "don't miss" destinations. Right from the day they poured their first glass of beer in the spring of 1989, this elegantly funky pub has been thronged with customers who discuss love, politics, sports and the character of the latest batch of bitter with equal passion. Even though Swans merits a visit just by being one of the very few brewpubs on the Island, that's just one of its many virtues. The creation of award-winning developer Michael Williams, the man who revived much of Victoria's "olde town" during the early 1980s, Swans is, not surprisingly, a superb mix of the old and the new. Williams took the historic shell of a turn-of-the-century feed warehouse/railway siding and renovated it with warmth and elegance. Its heavy-timbered post and beam construction and brick walls are lightened by stained glass, tile accents on a wood floor, and a painted, handmade bar fashioned by a Gulf Island artisan. Cultivated presentation—in the form of sprays of fresh flowers in the windows and enough contemporary paintings on the walls to outclass most of Victoria's art galleries—gives modern flair to a historic setting. Add in the good acoustics and a non-smoking nook and you get an almost unmatched venue in which to appreciate the brewmaster's art.

Swans is a combination pub/hotel/restaurant/brewery (tours can be arranged if you phone ahead and make arrangements with Sean the brewmaster), and its clientele includes downtown professionals, tourists and a cabal of bohemian artists who drop in once a week for their "swan dive." And what draws them, aside from all those great made-from-scratch beers, is the food. With a separate restaurant, you can expect more than just hamburgers; why not try the seafood brochette, the warm chicken walnut salad or one of the vegetarian dishes from the lunch menu? The "pub snacks" range from Swans Prawns and nachos to rum-glazed calypso ribs and Pandora's Camembert (which comes wrapped in bacon, with peach sauce). They even have fancy desserts, designer coffees and an impressive wine list (with a maximum corking fee of $10).

Whether you're hankering after a pint of bitter made "British style," or just want to sample the fine food and friendly atmosphere of a unique pub, you can't do better than a visit to Swans.

Island Trivia

Victoria's largest liquor firm was Pither and Leiser Ltd. Established in 1858, they had a plush, six-storey operation at the corner of Wharf and Fort. Following the creation of the Liquor Control Board in the 1920s, the building became an L.C.B. warehouse and also housed a liquor store until 1966.

The Garrick's Head

69 Bastion Square, Victoria
Telephone: 384-6835

Hours: 11 a.m. - 11 p.m., Monday - Saturday; 11 a.m. - 9 p.m., Sunday

The Navigator: Located right downtown, off Government Street in Bastion Square (just around from the Bedford Hotel).

Although downtown Victoria doesn't lack bars and beer parlours, there's a shortage of real neighbourhood pubs. **The Garrick's Head**, located in the heart of Old Town in Bastion Square, offers contemporary pub comfort in one of the city's most historic areas. The original Garrick's Head opened in 1867, when Victoria was a rough 'n' ready frontier town with mud streets, a small population . . and a disproportionately large number of grog shops. The first Garrick's was a saloon that specialized in whiskey instead of beer. Its location right across from the old courthouse meant that the men who were condemned to death by the judge got marched across the Square to Garrick's for a last drink before they swung. Although the historic buildings in Bastion Square—site of the original Fort Victoria—were restored and revived in the early 1970s, it wasn't until Labour Day of 1989 that Garrick's reopened, cast very much in the mould of the original. Oak beams, an unvarnished wood floor, teal blue wainscotting and tartan curtains help recall the spirit of the first Garrick's Head. A cosy fireplace and carriage lanterns on the wall complete the bygone mood.

"We're a neighbourhood pub in the downtown core," explains bartender Rob Wilkinson, who is proud of his friendly and generally quiet bar. The clientele tends to be mostly a business crowd during the day and after work, with more of a nightclub crowd showing up once the sun goes down. Beer gets served up in real "sleeves," and the taps dispense only the unpasteurized, locally made beer manufactured by Vancouver Island Brewery. The food here is fine as well (although longtime regulars lament the phasing out of the

16

garlic-laden hamburgers in favour of more ordinary ones). Aside from traditional pub fare, you can tuck into calamari, nachos or a raw veggie plate. And for that quintessential pub experience, order one of their huge, salty, chewy pretzels, which come with hot mustard and a guarantee that you'll be wanting yet another beer to wash it down with.

If you're looking for a laid-back bar where you can savour real beer—and maybe have a little shudder imagining which table the condemned men used to have their last drink at—then take your thirst in the direction of the Garrick's Head.

Island Trivia

Vork began on Fort Victoria in March, 1843. One hundred yards square, ʾe Fort was built on land now bounded by Government, Broughton, Wharf nd Bastion Streets.

Pub Philosopher

What contemptible scoundrel stole the cork from my lunch?"

— *W.C. Fields*

The Sticky Wicket

919 Douglas Street, Victoria
Telephone: 383-7137

Hours: 11:30 - 2:30, Monday - Saturday; 11:30 - midnight, Sunday

The Navigator: Right in downtown Victoria, corner of Douglas and Courtney.

With a name like **The Sticky Wicket** and an authentic English-red telephone booth plunked down on the sidewalk near the door, you'd be forgiven for assuming that this is merely the latest "olde England" pub to set up shop in Victoria. Truth is, there are no less than five bars doing a roaring trade behind that elegant green facade—to say nothing of the elevator and the open-air tennis court that help set this inimitable establishment apart from any other pub you're ever likely to hoist a tankard in.

Opened in June of 1990, this superb renovation to the Strathcona Hotel cost a cool $4 million, and much of that investment came from owner John Olson's spending spree in England, which resulted in a few container-loads of ornate fixtures, wood panelling and superb "heritage" bars that used to prop up patrons all over the British Isles. The centrepiece of The Sticky Wicket is a 120-year-old bar that did service on a nineteenth-century trans-Atlantic liner, then got shore leave to serve up Guinness by the gallon in Belfast. John paid $50,000 for this curved beauty, which now sits resplendent in the "Irish Bar" on the main floor.

The workmanship throughout The Sticky Wicket is simply wonderful: from the *faux* marble columns and the imported mahogany paneling (tended to by English craftsman Peter Carvell) to the baronial elegance of the chandeliers and the whimsy of a three-foot hanging clock designed like a pocket watch, this pub's a marvel. But don't waste all your time staring around: with more than a dozen import draught beers (including Harp Lager and Smithwicks) and a great kitchen, there are more immediate pleasures to attend to!

The menu, which comes on a cricket bat, includes everything from Holland sole and Cornish pasties to chicken fettucini and roast beef sandwiches. With a good selection of soups, salads and daily specials, it's no wonder that both the lunch and dinner trade here are wall to wall.

There are three bars on the main level (including the sports bar with four dart boards and three pool/billiards/snooker tables); a mezzanine section with fine window views and a kitchen that specializes in oriental stir-fries; and the seasonally open rooftop patio, where you can watch a tennis game, sip your beer and choose from salmon, chicken or hamburger on the barbecue.

With five different bars (all with varying brews on tap) and a great set of kitchens to keep your taste buds happy, The Sticky Wicket is the pub-lover's equivalent of one-stop shopping. Don't miss it!

Island Trivia

Although Rattenbury ran thirty-five percent over-budget when he built Victoria's Parliament Buildings, he did create a small boom in the process by using largely local materials, including Nelson Island granite, Haddington Island andesite, roof slates from Jarvis Inlet, and various native woods that were used to finish many of the rooms.

Fogg n' Suds

711 Broughton Street, Victoria
Telephone: 383-2337

Hours: 11 a.m. - 11 p.m., Monday - Thursday; 11 a.m. - 1 a.m., Friday - Saturday; 11 a.m. - 10 p.m., Sunday

The Navigator: Right in downtown Victoria, on Broughton between Douglas and Blanshard.

Although a restaurant chain would normally fall *way* outside the scope of a book on neighbourhood pubs, an exception has to be made when a business lives and breathes beer to the extent that **Fogg n' Suds** does. Imagine an uptown tavern with a few bistro touches and that's the flavour of this popular, high-energy bar. There are wood and wicker chairs, some upholstered booth and alcove seating, a few ceiling-scraping philodendrons and even some marble on the floor. With young, friendly help and contemporary sounds on the stereo, a lot of people gravitate here for good-time evenings. But for serious fans of blue-ribbon suds, it's the beer menu that will have your heart skipping a beat. Fogg boasts a veritable cornucopia of beer, with their cellar currently stocking over 250 bottled brands. They were also the first place to offer Guinness and other British and European delights when B.C. lifted its ban on draught imports in the summer of 1989. Currently, they've settled at an even dozen on the draught menu—typically including a roster of ten reliables such as Warsteiner, Double Diamond and Smithwicks and a pair of special imports that gets changed regularly.

If challenged to list his most outrageous beers, the manager will likely become nearly euphoric. Maybe he'll rave about the Liefmans Kriek, a Belgian Trappist ale flavoured with macerated cherries (but bring all your thirsty friends—this only comes in nine-litre bottles and costs a cool $300). Then there's a lower-chakra form of enlightenment that comes via India, courtesy of its Gur Lager. If you want to try a beer that bites back, try arm-wrestling the world's two strongest beers, Eku 28 and Samichlaus. (The latter

20

is brewed once-yearly on December 6, then laid down for a full year prior to bottling. But be prepared to drop $8.95 to find out what fourteen percent beer tastes like.) And connoisseurs with truly deep wallets can have the sommelier present an Edelfuerfest; this "cognac of beers," which comes in rare vintages, costs nearly $2 an ounce.

Serious drinkers can join up with the 20,000 active members of Fogg's "passport club," getting their passports stamped to record their thirst-quenching world travels as they sample beers from places as exotic as the Amazon and Papua New Guinea.

Remember, however, that because Fogg is a restaurant, drinking patrons are required to buy some food along with their brew. Luckily, that's not a problem: aside from award-winning nachos and burgers, they have non-pub fare such as calamari, spaghetti and ribs, and a chicken stir-fry. And if you want the true beer-drinking experience, order one of their handmade pretzels, coated in thirst-inducing rock salt.

The racing scull above the bar is a reminder of Fogg's corporate support of the world-class rowing teams at UVic. They also turn the place over to a bunch of jazz crazies in July during the ten-day JazzFest. But mostly, you'll cherish Fogg n' Suds as a true shrine to man's first potent potable.

Beer Trivia
German Pilsner, the benchmark lager against which all others are judged, was first brewed in 1292.

Pub Philosopher
"I really don't drink, but I'll split a quart with you."
— *Johnston Peter*

Oxford Arms Pub

301 Oxford Street, Victoria
Telephone: 382-3301

Hours: 11 a.m. - 11 p.m., daily

The Navigator: Near Beacon Hill Park, in the Cook Street
                    Village, at the corner of Cook and Oxford Street.

Although the **Oxford Arms** is the second-newest pub in this book, it is even more noteworthy as an interesting example of the ongoing politics of pubbing. For months and months, would-be publican Harry Lucas kept pushing for a neighbourhood pub in the village on lower Cook Street, and it took two hotly contested referendums and a subsequent court challenge before the loud chorus of dismay—What about noise? What about parking problems? What about drunk drivers?—could be muted sufficiently for the pub proposal to squeak by. Opened in November of 1990, the pub's food and ambience instantly made it one of the most popular spots in the neighbourhood (and many of the pub's more vocal opponents were quick to venture in, happy to wash down their humble pie with a pint of the various fine beers on tap). So while there is still an obvious need for some good public relations to convince people that the appropriate pub can be an asset to any neighbourhood, it's also clear that a sensibly run establishment can turn suspicious mutterings into sighs of pleasure.

Too new to have acquired any quirks, the Oxford Arms is a tasteful neo-British pub complete with oak flooring, Tiffany lamps, mahogany wainscotting, "marbled" wallpaper, old-fashioned ceiling fans, large plants and brass rails. An eight-foot stained glass dome (locally made) commands the ceiling, while a fireplace will take the winter chill off any of the numerous walk-in customers. The pub is one large space, sectioned by half-walls. The tables are often full, so those vigorous of limb may find themselves propped up at the island near the bar, boot on the brass foot-rail and beer in hand.

Comfortable if unremarkable in appearance, the Oxford Arms is saved from a handsome blandness by the vitality of the clientele

22

no pub around has a more interesting mix of people. Little old ladies tucking into salads, brawny working-class lads exercising their elbows with a succession of frosty pints, black-clad bohemian artists, young professional women discussing life at the legal bar—the Oxford is a true microcosm of one the most distinctive neighbourhoods in Victoria. It also benefits from a cosy yet uncrowded feeling, and one of the better kitchens you'll find on a Victoria pub tour.

Set right in the heart of the Cook Street Village, the Oxford Arms is as pedestrian-oriented an establishment as you'll find in all of Victoria, and one that serves a distinctive and varied community. Its food, service and happy clientele pretty well sum up all that's good about neighbourhood pubs.

Beer Trivia

"Ye people of Canada listen
I've something I want you to hear
There's trouble in store for our nation
Because of the whiskey and beer

It hinders our moral advancement
It menaces every home
It fills every soul with its ragings
Who drinks of the poisonous foam
　　　　— Nineteenth-century Canadian Temperance tune

Christie's Carriage House Pub

1739 Fort Street, Victoria
Telephone: 598-5333

Hours: 11 a.m. - 11 p.m., Monday - Sunday

The Navigator: On the south side of Fort Street, between Oak Bay Junction and Richmond.

Although Victoria has more than its fair share of fine pubs in the "Olde England" style, the best one is an authentic heritage house that recreates turn-of-the-century Victoria with charm, flair and comfort. **Christie's Carriage House Pub** was built around 1898 by Elbridge Christie, a renowned carriage maker. Exquisitely rendered in the ornate Queen Anne style—characterized by its fancy shingling and a flamboyant roofline incorporating gables and towers—"Sandolphon," as the house was known, was long a Victoria landmark. Even though Christie left the city in 1909, after sensing that the carriage trade was doomed by a new-fangled contraption called the automobile, the house stayed in the family till 1948. Latterly, it was subdivided into apartments and almost fell to the wrecker's ball; it was salvaged by astute business interests in the 1980s, and by 1986 a gorgeously restored Christie's opened for business. (Two carriages, including a 1905 Rockaway Coupe, stand near the pub entrance as a reminder of the building's past.)

Spiffed up in high Edwardian fashion—with dark woods, stained glass, brass rails, a patterned ceiling designed in "stamped foil" and wallpaper striped as authoritatively as a banker's shirt—Christie's accurately recreates the lush comforts that Elbridge and his family knew. These days, of course, you need neither a tie nor an invitation to dine at the Christies' . . . and the opportunity should not be passed up! The kitchen in this fine establishment is one of its main drawing cards; from pub classics such as fish and chips to more contemporary fare like chicken tenderloin stir-fry, Christie's offers up a generous plate of quality food at a reasonable price. They also offer wine by the glass and have so many beers on tap—including an "import draught of the month"—that they offer cheap beer "tasters" for unsure sippers.

Although essentially a true neighbourhood pub ("We get a lot of regulars in here," notes a long-term waitress), Christie's draws trade from all over the city. It's a lively place, but rugs and other fabrics soften the buzz of happy conversation. Essentially designed on an open plan, there are several half-walls that create a variety of nooks and crannies that can accommodate various social needs. So whether you've dropped in for a romantic chat in a cushiony corner or want some spirited fellowship with the Monday night dart team, Christie's Carriage House offers old-fashioned comfort and the pleasures of sweet company.

Island Trivia

From early on, Oak Bay and the Uplands were identified as a posh social enclave. Streetcar passengers en route to the Uplands had to have passes proving that they were residents or visiting someone.

Pub Philosopher

"There is nothing which has yet been contrived by man, by which so much happiness is produced as by a good tavern or inn."
                                                                    — *Samuel Johnson*

The George and Dragon

1302 Gladstone Avenue, Victoria
Telephone: 388-4458

Hours: 10:00 a.m. - midnight, daily

The Navigator: Right at the corner of Gladstone and Fernwood.

Billed as a "pub-style restaurant," **The George and Dragon** is a very welcome addition to Fernwood. Replacing the largely unlamented Fernwood Inn, this brand-new establishment is a lively and hip destination in one of Victoria's most distinctive neighbourhoods. Although Fernwood itself is experiencing its own share of renovation and change, it is nothing like what went into rehabilitating the old Inn. After steam cleaning away years of grime (and scraping off the world's ugliest orange wall-to-wall carpet), the eight new owners set to with paint and wallpaper. Decorator Hannah Kirkham, whose credentials include Christie's and Maude Hunter's, helped give the renovation some finesse and a genuine pub pedigree. Ale aficionados will feel immediately at home with the post and beam construction, elegant wallpaper, Tiffany lamps, antique floral prints and artful array of books and steins along shelves just below the ceiling.

Overseeing the culinary action is chef Herb Rose, lately of Chauney's, who brings polish and care to the many dishes that compose the well-considered menu. This is a fine lunch spot—the soups are excellent—while both the lunch and dinner specials would be at home in a fancy restaurant. (On one visit, while I was happily tucking into my prawn and pasta dinner, somebody in the next booth purred to her companion: "This Caesar is *good.*")

The Dragon is definitely Fernwood's social centre-cum-nightclub, and there's an emphasis placed on quality entertainment. Aside from occasional appearances by the likes of Brazilian guitar wizard Celso Machado, there's a regular blues jam on Thursday nights, while the music on the weekend ranges from straight-ahead jazz to barrelhouse blues . . . with a little stand-up comedy thrown in for good measure. "It's whatever it takes to make this a fun place to come to," states co-owner Allan Sproule. With his and brother

Dale's background as owners of the Juan de Fuca Whalers hockey club (they sold it in 1988), it's not surprising that the new pub is happy to sponsor everything from field hockey teams to croquet tournaments. But notwithstanding all the sports support and uptown entertainment, much of the trade at this handsome pub is local. "This is a real neighbourhood place," says Allan, noting that a lot of people like to walk here. "Some come from up to a mile away, just to get some exercise," he adds.

Whether you want to hear some great music or treat yourself to a fine dinner before ambling across the road to take in the latest play at the Belfry Theatre, a visit to Fernwood isn't really complete without a stopover at the friendly George and Dragon.

Pub Philosopher

"There are, I believe, some of you who never touch alcohol. I respect your convictions. But I am sorry for you at the same time. Because when you wake up in the morning, that's as good as you're ever gonna feel."
— *Robert Mitchum, addressing a large group*

The Snug

Oak Bay Beach Hotel
1175 Beach Drive, Victoria
Telephone: 598-4556

Hours: 11:00 a.m. - midnight, Monday - Saturday; noon - 9:00 p.m., Sunday

The Navigator: Take Oak Bay Avenue through the Village to Windsor Avenue and turn left. Go right on Beach Drive. The Oak Bay Beach Hotel is two blocks up on the sea side.

In a city renowned for its quaintness and Old World charms, few places embody that sense of character as elegantly as the Oak Bay Beach Hotel, a picturesque Tudor palace that was painstakingly restored after a disastrous fire in 1930. And one of the best places to savour the unique pleasures of this seaside establishment is in its cosy lounge, appropriately known as **The Snug**.

English pubs traditionally had a small room reserved for privileged patrons who, for various reasons, did not want to be spotted with an incriminating glass in their hands. This "snug" would have a diverse clientele: the local bobby on his rounds might slip by for a thirst-slaking pint in between capturing crooks, while the vicar would be glad for a sip of sherry away from the disapproving scowl of his housekeeper. These rooms tended to become like exclusive clubs, and strangers were rarely made to feel welcome.

Such is certainly not the case in Victoria's "snug," which has retained that sense of historic appeal but dispensed with the snobbery. With its hand-adzed black posts and beams, brick and plaster walls, leaded windows and garland of beer steins above the bar, Oak Bay's most senior drinking establishment is a classic example of a British pub at its old-fashioned, friendly best. Long known as "duffle coat heaven"—a wry tribute to the university students and their even tweedier professors who come here in great numbers to pursue non-academic studies—this bar has a confiden and outgoing air, as befits its location in such a posh pocket of Victoria. Along with the university crowd, the hotel's international clientele and drop-ins from nearby Uplands and Oak Bay guarantee that there's lots of urbane chatter over cocktails.

During summer, try for a verandah table in order to better savour the stunning view. The Snug is sited at the juncture of the Straits of Georgia and Juan de Fuca, and the beguiling marine vista also embraces nearby Discovery Island and the more distant San Juans, while snow-capped Mount Baker completes the picture-postcard scene. With seabirds or eagles drifting through the blue skies, and the Oak Bay Beach Hotel's own ships heading out on lunch charters or in search of trophy salmon, you'll find that it's all too easy to let an hour or two slip away as you get caught up in the quiet rhythms of this fine bar.

Add in the deft service and the truly fine food—the chef puts on all the regular pub fare as well as a baron of beef, halibut steak and savoury treats such as Scotch eggs—and it's easy to figure out why so many customers from all over the city make this their "local." Anyone seeking Old World ambience in a quintessential West Coast setting need look no further than the Snug.

Beer Trivia

Some Temperance propagandists tried to scare off boozers by spreading the lurid story that heavy drinkers sometimes burst into flames, literally becoming human candles as a result of spontaneous combustion.

29

The Barley Mow Pub

2581 Penrhyn Street, Victoria
Telephone: 477-4412

Hours: 11:30 a.m. - midnight, Monday - Saturday; 11:30 a.m. - 10:00 p.m., Sunday

The Navigator: Located right in the heart of Cadboro Bay village, on the water side, just down the hill from the University of Victoria.

Located just a thought-filled stroll down the hill from the University of Victoria, **The Barley Mow** is one of the most distinctive pubs in all of Victoria. Its architecture is a striking mix of traditional Tudor and a contemporary West Coast sensibility. With post and beam construction, half-timbered plaster walls, peaked roof, leaded windows and an array of British flags, there's no mistaking the primary design influence. And the name itself, which refers to a harvest of the barley used to make almost all beers, is a common pub appellation in Britain. Yet architect Nigel Banks added in some strange angles and a two-storey layout featuring a rectangular atrium that allows the maximum visual connection between both levels. Garlands of ivy drift languorously out of large copper pots, while a double-decker brick fireplace keeps both levels warm in winter. And during summer some of the best times are available outside, both on the second-storey balcony or at one of the tables set up outside the main entrance.

Before the Barley Mow became a pub in 1987, it had a restaurant licence, and that legacy of fine food has continued. Although the standard pub fare is impeccable, the regulars here will typically pounce when their favourite special comes through on its latest rotation. And those seeking some late-night carbohydrates might want to check out the delicious nachos. The beverage menu is equally satisfying, with six beers and two ciders on tap (bottled beer fanciers can choose from among Weinhard's Dark, Pilsener Urquell and McEwans). The margaritas are made with real lime juice, not from those pernicious glow-in-the-dark mixes. And thanks to th

influence of a longtime waiter (and part-time screen writer), the drink specials are named after David Lynch movies: there's nothing like a "Wild At Heart," a "Blue Velvet" or the obliterating "Eraserhead" to help you recover from a rough day at the office!

Intimate and friendly, the Barley Mow is a fascinating microcosm of the Cadboro Bay area: university types may be discussing the prospects of different career paths at one table, while the retirees next to them lament sagging house prices in the Uplands or out at Ten Mile Point. But just when the references to Hegelian dialectics and leveraged buyouts get a tad thick, some local lager laddies in T-shirts will mosey down beside the bar and fill the air with *real* darts instead of just verbal ones.

Sitting in the shadow of one of the country's most attractively manicured universities (don't miss a visit to its fabulous rhododendron gardens), and just one minute's walk from a great beach and park, the Barley Mow makes the perfect rest stop after an amble through scenic Cadboro Bay. If you're hungry or thirsty, don't hesitate to let them welcome you with friendly service and their uniquely West Coast charms.

Beer Trivia

Smuggler's Cove earned its name as one of the favourite launch points for smugglers ferrying liquor across the Strait of Juan de Fuca to the American speakeasies.

The Monkey Tree Pub

4025 Borden Street
Telephone: 727-3550

Hours: 11:00 a.m. - midnight, Monday - Saturday; 11:00 a.m. - 11:00 p.m., Sunday

The Navigator: Follow Quadra out of town. At the McKenzie intersection, turn right and then a quick left at the next traffic lights (Borden Street). Pub is 100 metres up on the right.

Opened in September of 1986, **The Monkey Tree** is one of Victoria's first real neighbourhood pubs. There's an undeniable British feel to this attractive bar, what with the leaded windows, half-curtains, ornate brass lights and elegant millwork executed in blond wood. Some old-style prints on the wall and two floor-to-ceiling bookshelves complete the sense that you're paying a visit to an Edwardian study. But instead of sipping on sherry, better check out the beer list: aside from a half-dozen beers on tap there are thirty import bottled beers available, from countries as diverse as China, Brazil and the Phillipines. (And scotch drinkers can choose from among seventeen malts that stand tall at the handsome wood-pillared bar.)

Despite its city-wide reputation, the Monkey Tree is predominantly a place where the "locals" come and drink. There's a real mix of people who come here—university students, workers, older folks—but most of them have lots of energy to burn: this is the place to show up for an exuberant good time. Friendly staff and cosy seating (and a crackling fireplace during winter) make this a fine place to meet your friends . . . or make new ones.

While owners Gordon Card and Bill Beadle sponsor baseball and basketball teams, a lot of other athletes consider the bar their informal home as well. Lacrosse teams get rid of their thirsts here on Wednesday nights, and the regular baseball tournaments at nearby Reynolds School typically culminate in a post-game analysis over several jugs of draught.

Food is definitely part of the winning formula at this popular

pub. The Monkey Tree does a big lunch trade, and business people on the fast track often invest in the "Quick Lunch" special, an ever-changing soup and salad combo. The burgers are always in demand, and the enchiladas and dry pepper wings are perennial best sellers. And Sunday brunch traditionalists won't want to miss out on their savoury Eggs Benedict.

Next time you're puzzling over where to go for good food and good times, quit scratching your head and make a direct path to the Monkey Tree Pub.

Pub Philosopher

"When I am in really great trouble, as anyone who knows me intimately will tell you, I refuse everything except food and drink."

— *Oscar Wilde*

Maude Hunter's Neighbourhood Pub

3810 Shelbourne Street
Telephone: 721-2337

Hours: 11:30 - midnight, Monday - Saturday; 11:30 - 11:00 p.m., Sunday

The Navigator: Maude Hunter's is on Shelbourne Street, just 100 metres north (Mount Douglas side) of the Cedar Hill intersection.

As Victoria began to make the slow shift from over-sized beer barns to the more intimate comforts of neighbourhood pubs, **Maude Hunter's** quickly provided convincing evidence that there was a market hungry for good food and good beer in a pleasing environment. Maude's was bustling with patrons right from its opening day in 1986, and has continued to remain one of the most popular neighbourhood pubs in the city. It's not hard to figure out why.

The post and beam construction is in the best of British pub traditions, as are the leaded windows, brass rails, brocade-covered alcove seating, plants and ornate brass lamps. Worth a glance or two are the books, mugs and other memorabilia that wend their way along the elaborate moulding near the ceiling, as well as the old-fashioned art adorning the walls. A corner-mounted fireplace, right next to where food orders are placed, provides a cosy focus when Victoria gets damp and inward-looking during those November downpours and drizzles. Not meant to be a slavish copy of an Edwardian pub, Maude's puts its emphasis on conviviality and comfort—thus maintaining the traditions of the original Maude Hunter, whose turn-of-the-century corner store served as this neighbourhood's original meeting place for a few decades (Although it's safe to say that the original Maude, an outspoken prohibitionist, would be more than a little chagrined to find herself the figurehead of a grog shop!)

But even with all that demon drink so readily available even Mrs. Hunter would have to agree that the happy buzz of conversation always in evidence at this pub is precisely what any real neighbourhood needs. For this is definitely a place where the locals come to relax, triumphant in their leisure. Whether indulging in scandal-swapping conversation, absorbed in a game of chess or happily sharing a generous plate of nachos, the patrons here seem to share some inside tip on how to have a good time. Much of the "secret" of Maude's is the food, of course. Generous portions of consistently tasty pub fare have guaranteed a booming lunch trade, while a lot of people will head this way for a treat when the dinner bell goes and they're just too harried to bother banging around with their own pots and pans.

Popular enough to be called a "neighbourhood" pub for the entire Victoria area, Maude Hunter's offers cordial comforts and fine fare sufficient to charm even the most ardent temperance advocate.

Beer Trivia

The world's largest collection of beer mats is owned by Leo Pisker of Vienna, Austria . . . but don't get him started on the subject, because he has 130,600 different mats to show you, collected from 153 different countries.

Pub Philosopher

"If the headache would only precede the intoxication, alcoholism would be a virtue."

— Samuel Butler

35

The Bird of Paradise

4291 Glanford Avenue
Telephone: 727-6466

Hours: 11 a.m. - 11 p.m., daily

The Navigator: Follow Quadra out of town, turning left onto Mackenzie Avenue, then right onto Glanford (at the lights). Follow along for a couple of miles; the pub is on the right as you come within viewing distance of Broadmead.

On the principle of saving (one of) the best for last, **The Bird of Paradise** opened for business just a couple of weeks before this book was going to the printers. Proudly sited in a 1914 Royal Oak farmhouse that's been tastefully renovated and expanded, the theme for the Paradise was inspired by the earthy monochromes of the American Southwest; thanks to superb design sense and a lot of attention to detail, it makes a uniquely beautiful option for Island beer sippers who can't afford a vacation in Arizona.

"I didn't want just another oak and brass-type pub," says owner Diego Trozzo. "The Santa Fe style is warm and comfortable . . . and it's also more authentically North American." The sandy-pink walls of textured terra cotta make a pleasing backdrop for a gallery-quality collection of hand-painted ceramics, Mexican woven rugs and some striking Navajo pots made from sticks and palm husks. Cactuses and other greenery are spotted throughout while the rattan furniture boasts geometrically patterned cushions coloured with desert pastels.

The first thing to note on entering is the semi-circular bar, which is a stunner. The east side of the pub, which overlooks Broadmead and Christmas Hill, features a glassed-in rotunda complete with french doors opening onto a summer-time patio. Over to the west side, the mood tends to be more cosy and private, with a nook and fireplace. A tiddly JBL sound system, complete with subwoofer, plays uptown tunes from the likes of the Neville Brothers and Peter Gabriel.

The excellent menu, although partly reflecting regional cuisine isn't just a selection of Tex-Mex tongue torchers. Aside from variety of chicken and   beef burgers, there are treats like the Moroccan chicken salad sandwich or the scallops and prawns grandly reposing in a savoury peanut-curry sauce. The list of gourmet pub snacks includes baked camembert, squid and garlic toast. And the beer menu is equally attractive: aside from a selection of big-label beers, fans of more handmade brews can get a mugful of Hermann's or Okanagan Spring Pale Ale to wash down those nachos with.

Even though he opened less than a month ago, Diego is already sponsoring a mixed slow-pitch team and expects to be part of the dart league circuit before long. A slightly raised area at one end of the pub will act as a stage for occasional entertainment, which will range from live music to stand-up comedy. And bird watchers can get a unique treat here: Diego's hand-raised flock of peacocks wanders about the grounds, preening ambassadors to this delightful pub.

There's no need to hassle over overbooked flights to Santa Fe, now that the Bird of Paradise combines the pleasures of the exotic with the comforts of home.

Island Trivia

The local Songhees Indians helped cut the twenty-two-foot cedar pickets used for Fort Victoria's stockade, earning one blanket for every forty pickets they produced.

The Prairie Inn

7806 E. Saanich Road, Victoria
Telephone: 652-1575

Hours: 11 a.m. - midnight, Sunday - Thursday; 11 a.m. - 1 a.m., Friday - Saturday.

The Navigator: From Victoria, take Highway 17 north towards Sidney; turn west at Mt. Newton X-Road (opposite Waddling Dog Inn). The Prairie Inn is 1 km along, at the first stop sign.

Despite those satellite dishes perched up on the roof, **The Prairie Inn** harks back to Victoria's frontier days, when publican Henry Simpson (who had long since been slaking the local thirst with his "Prairie Tavern") built himself a hotel in 1893. This wooden landmark has gone on to house a store, a rooming house, a cafe and, since 1974, the neighbourhood pub.

Although the locals most appreciate the Prairie Inn for its friendly atmosphere (and the incredible food, at low, near-frontier prices), beer lovers should note that this was the first establishment on the Island to get a "brewpub" licence, way back in 1982.

Brian Mayze has been the brewmaster here for six years, and he uses an unhopped malt extract so that he can fine-tune the flavour of the three in-house beers, which include an Australian-style lager and a "black bitter." Unlike the brewmasters at Spinnakers and Swans, who are strongly influenced by standard English beer-making tradition, Brian crafts a more mainstream product. "Our beers are colder and more carbonated—that's the Canadian style," he explains. "Because we use no chemicals or preservatives, we're essentially offering an all-natural alternative to the commercial beers such as Molson's." Brian estimates that their brewery turns out more than 15,000 gallons a year. "We have the most draught sales of any neighbourhood pub in B.C.," he says proudly.

And once you've had a mug of that high-quality lager, it will be time to take your measure of the menu. With a dozen dinners to choose from—everything from baked sole and tender N.Y. steaks to

those aptly named "belly buster" burgers—the Prairie Inn menu is hard to top. And keep in mind that the only thing small about the meals here is the price . . . so patrons wishing a lighter bite should maybe stick to the snack list, which includes oysters, pocket pizzas, zucchini sticks and nachos.

So, if you want a beer and a bite (well . . . *numerous* bites) in a real community-oriented pub, then head towards the Prairie Inn. Whether you end up quaffing an ale in the sports nook or tucking into a juicy steak in the more old-fashioned section of the pub, you'll be the latest in a century-old tradition of satisfied customers.

Beer Trivia

In ancient Babylon, female brewers were temple priestesses.

The Brig Marine Pub

7172 Brentwood Drive, Victoria
Telephone: 652-2413

Hours:　　　　　11 a.m. - 11:45 p.m. daily

The Navigator:　Take West Saanich Road to Brentwood. Turn left onto Verdier Avene, then left again onto Brentwood Drive. The Inn is right beside the Brentwood Bay/Mill Bay ferry dock.

The Brig was Victoria's first marine pub, and it's aptly situated in the Brentwood Inn Resort complex, which offers cruising and fishing charters, a sixty-berth marina and a waterview motel with full-facility units. Whether you arrive by land or by sea, are looking for a light bite or dinner and overnight accommodation, you'll be in good hands at The Brig.

Overlooking scenic Saanich Inlet, with sufficient moorage to divert any dockwatcher, this popular marine pub has an obvious appeal for passing yachtsmen, who often drop by to shower up and then linger over a few brews while their gamey, sea-going togs get de-salinated in the downstairs laundromat. But despite the water location, The Brig has loads of appeal for mere landlubbers, as testified to by the rack of softball trophies and a large number of repeat drop-ins from town. There is also a brisk tourist trade from nearby Butchart Gardens.

The Inn's Oak and Barrel Restaurant lures customers from all over Central and North Saanich, and a lot of that magic has rubbed off on the adjoining pub kitchen, which turns out excellent food. The meals range from classic pub fare such as burgers, fish and chips and shepherd's pie to trendier noshes such as zucchini cuts, chicken wings, potato skins, taco salad and pasta.

As befits a marine pub with prime waterside views, there is a recently upgraded outdoor deck, which flies its jauntily coloured sun umbrellas till October. Also new in 1990 is the glass-walled sunroom, which offers year-round comfort and the best in dockwatching diversions.

For decades now the Brentwood Inn has run a fishing charter service, with a fleet of boats that has reaped a bountiful harvest of prime West Coast salmon. Not to be left behind on shore, Brig owner Michael Keepence christened the fifty-four-foot *Sea Jac* motor yacht and initiated his own line of afternoon and dinner cruises, complete with a tuxedo-clad bartender. The Jac is also chartered for birthdays, office parties and weddings: many a pub patron has had the chance to see a bride skipping down the dock in her wedding whites, ready for a uniquely romantic adventure.

Beer Trivia

During the Middle Ages there were frequent pirate attacks on the port of Hamburg, whose primary export was beer. During one assault the pirates got what they came for . . . and then some. In a neat twist, the defenders poured thousands of gallons of boiling beer down on the heads of that scurvy lot.

Pub Philosopher

"He talked with more claret than clarity."

— Susan Ertz

The Rumrunner

9881 Seaport Place, Victoria
Telephone: 656-5643

Hours: 11 a.m. - midnight, seven days a week

The Navigator: Head out the Pat Bay Highway towards the ferries, turn right at Sidney's Beacon Avenue; just before the end, turn left onto Seaport Place.

Themed in honour of legendary local rumrunner Johnny Schnarr (currently a law-abiding ninety-six-year-old), **The Rumrunner** is a brand new marine pub that is a uniquely attractive addition to the burgeoning town of Sidney. Note the carved wooden sign as you approach the pub: it was designed by *Times-Colonist* cartoonist Adrian Raeside. Inside, the room is commanded by a handsome three-sided bar, stained mahogany red, which boasts a frieze of stained glass illustrating the rumrunning exploits of Johnny. Grab a glass of thoroughly legal hooch and then take a gander at all the period photos on the walls: they provide fascinating glimpses back into the Roaring Twenties, when a not-so-staid Victoria kept Seattle's speakeasies awash in thousands of gallons of good Canadian whiskey. (Sidney resident Bill Armson, who was one of the area's youngest "runners," came in to check out the bar one day and recognized himself toting a case of grog in one of the old photos; look for his proud autograph.)

Although The Rumrunner has an elegant Edwardian feel, it has cleverly sidestepped the brass-and-blond-wood cliches in favour of sponge-painted walls (resembling marbled endpapers in antique books) and subtle design touches and colour accents on the blinds and furniture. Masculine and warm, the place has been a well-deserved hit ever since it opened. "We're publicans, in the old-fashioned sense of the word," declares Bill Singer, who opened the place along with partner Michael Bullock, both of whom are fondly remembered from earlier days at the Oak Bay Snug (Bill was a waiter there for thirteen years, while Michael was the food and beverage manager for the hotel). These two gentlemen have clearly created a labour of love

Their talented chef is Paul Lum, also of the Oak Bay Beach Hotel, and he serves a fine selection of snacks and meals that many restaurants would be jealous of. Soups include a hearty french onion and a seafood special that changes daily. Aside from finger foods like onion rings, chicken strips and nachos, there's heartier fare such as burgers, fish and chips, steak sandwiches and a good catch of seafood. Pay attention to the board posted at the door on the way in, as the daily specials are always worth a try.

Sited next to Sidney Pier, in a great harbour that's been nicely landscaped, The Rumrunner offers both superb water views and easy access to American boaters. While Mount Baker provides a natural focal point for window-side tipplers and anyone sampling the sea air out on the red-bricked patio, luckier customers might get to see eagles fishing for salmon, migrating orca pods or even a gray whale cavorting offshore.

Bike racks, easy handicapped access, and an adjoining restaurant suitable for children are a few of the little extras that should induce almost anyone with a thirst that it's time to do a little "rumrunning."

Beer Trivia

During American Prohibition, Canadian rumrunners did their part to keep their fellow drinkers happy south of the border. Although it wasn't against Canadian laws to ship booze, captains were required to declare where their cargo was headed. Often, dummy destinations were listed to satisfy this formality, and one tiny but well-sited island regularly received hundreds of cases of liquor — presumably a tribute to the prodigious thirst of its sole occupant, a lighthouse keeper!

Blue Peter Pub and Restaurant

2270 Harbour Road, Sidney
Telephone: 656-4551

Hours: Noon - 11:00 p.m., Sunday - Wednesday; 11:30 - midnight, Thursday - Saturday; (shorter hours and closed Mondays during offseason)

The Navigator: From the Pat Bay Highway, turn right onto Beacon Avenue in Sidney. Turn left at Resthaven Drive and follow along for a few miles. Turn right at Harbour Road (look for the "Blue Peter" sign) and continue for a few hundred metres.

Named after an international yachting flag that signals when a ship is about to set sail, the **Blue Peter** signals maritime pleasures to those who have just returned from some wave-tossed sailing or fishing adventure . . . and functions as an equally attractive destination for those who wish to retain their landlubber status. This marine pub and restaurant overlooking Sidney's Tsehum Harbour was opened in May of 1986, and the Blue Peter immediately established itself as a casual and friendly place with loads of contemporary West Coast appeal. The off-white and blue-grey colour scheme makes an appropriate backdrop for the yachting pennants and sailboat art on the walls, while several canvas sails form a criss-crossed canopy on the ceiling. Hardwood floors, wicker furniture and lots of green plants are a seductive invitation for customers to spend a few hours relaxing over a beer and chatting about their new Genoa sail or the trophy coho they're about to catch. The dock-side windows offer great views of all the wharfed boats, but there's nothing like a stroll to feel the breeze on your cheeks, or maybe catch sight of a seabird diving for his dinner. This fine marine pub also functions as a bit of an art gallery—they feature a half-dozen local artists, whose work is on sale.

The kitchen here is very much worth consulting. There's an interesting "snack" menu available throughout the day (nachos

potato skins, home-cut fries, Cajun shrimp) and a fuller menu available during dinner hours. And if the fettucini, salmon filet, chicken salad or various sandwiches aren't quite posh enough, you can always saunter into the adjoining restaurant where an expanded menu offers gourmet entrees.

Although this pub doesn't cater much to the tourist trade—it's largely a meeting place for the area's local fishermen, boatbuilders and retirees—everyone is made to feel welcome indeed. The dress "code" embraces anything from jeans and L.L. Bean outdoor gear to fancy togs, and most of the customers have that healthy and hearty look that comes with a love of the sea and the outdoors. The attached marina has about forty permanent slips, with only four spaces right in front of the pub that are available for transients (if you want to arrive via water, it's a good idea to phone ahead). But whether you arrive on a sailboat or a pair of roller skates, the Blue Peter will pipe you aboard with genuine West Coast friendliness.

Beer Trivia

In London in 1814 a huge vat of Porter burst, releasing nearly a million gallons; this ocean of beer flooded the nearby tenement houses, killing eight people.

The Stonehouse Pub

2215 Canoe Cove, Sidney
Telephone: 656-3498

Hours: 11 a.m. - 11 p.m., daily

The Navigator: Head down the Pat Bay Highway towards the
                    Swartz Bay Ferry Terminal. Turn right just before
                    the ferries, following the signs to Canoe Cove.

The Stonehouse Pub, one of Victoria's most beautiful
shrines to the brewer's art, was originally a private, Tudor-style
home that was erected by master boatbuilder Hugh Rodd in the
1930s. Its steep gables and leaded windows recall the homes in
southern England—a fact that wasn't lost on expatriate British
hotelier Simon Deane, who transformed the private home into a
public house in the mid-1980s.

The Stonehouse is at its most expansive during summer,
when the outdoor patio, dotted with colourful sun umbrellas,
gives patrons a chance to relax and admire the well-tended
gardens and lawns. Inside, the pub conversion has left the house
largely unchanged: the dining room, the pub and the conservatory
offer three distinctive venues in which to quaff a pint and make
the acquaintance of one of the Island's finest menus. Simon
ensures that everything is fresh-cooked and homemade (the lunch
and dinner specials are always a good bet), with regular
selections ranging from roast beef and salmon steak to such
traditional fare as a ploughman's lunch. This old-fashioned
publican has noted with satisfaction that the trend is towards
buying food instead of just drinking. "When we first opened, beer
sales were close to seventy per cent of our take," he notes. "Today
food sales are considerably above beer purchases." Which isn't to
say that the beer menu isn't exceptional: aside from a cooler full of
import bottled beer, they sell draught Guinness and Stone
Yorkshire Bitter at bargain prices, as well as offering the full
selection of excellent ales and lagers made locally by the
Vancouver Island Brewing Company.

Simon is quite a sports fan, and he plays on both the cricket and croquet teams that his pub sponsors. The Stonehouse's two lawns are set up for croquet from June through September, and Simon takes the game with fair seriousness: he plays six-wicket international style (the sets are worth $2,000 a pop), and his team has toured as far as San Francisco, where they competed in the U.S. Open. Although the pub has been croquet-mad since 1986, the cricketers just got going in 1990—and made the playoffs in their Island-based twelve-league circuit in their first year! (Word is that the other teams had better watch out.)

Although summer offers the best time for a stroll to take in the sights of the nearby Canoe Cove Marina, the damp days of winter are not without their own special pleasures: that's when fireplaces and stoves impart a homey cosiness to all three rooms at The Stonehouse—doubtless one of the reasons many of the locals drop by in the off-season to play cards over a pint. Winter is also the time for their occasional special events, such as Medieval Night, which includes both jesters and higher-born folk in a droll and frisky frolic.

For pleasure and comfort in a distinguished pub environment, winter or summer, it's hard to top The Stonehouse.

Beer Trivia

During the days of yore when serious drinking was a matter of pride, vessels could be hefty indeed; they commonly included tankards with a two-quart capacity, while some held up to two gallons.

Pub Philosopher

A woman drove me to drink, and I never even had the courtesy to thank her."
— *W.C. Fields*

Port-of-Call

Tudor House Hotel
533 Admirals Road, Victoria
Telephone: 389-9943

Hours: 11:30 a.m. - 1:30 a.m., Monday - Saturday; 11:00 a.m. - midnight, Sunday

The Navigator: From downtown Victoria take the Johnson Street Bridge and follow Esquimalt Road for 4.5 km. The Tudor House is easy to spot on the corner of Esquimalt and Admirals Roads.

Although many a beer-sozzled old-timer will remember how raunchy the Tudor House Hotel used to be, it's been nearly a decade since a mighty renovation gave new life to the **Port-of-Call** transforming grime into grandeur. Although the place still resembles a castle from the outside, the inside is anything but dim and medieval. Two fancy bars, elaborated with carved wood, brass and leaded glass, set an uptown mood. Other fancy touches include square posts that are mirrored, lots of plants, a cosy gas fireplace and Tiffany lamps. But—ever mindful that this bar has served as the "local" for Canada's western naval port of Naden for more than a half-century—most of the decoration establishes a maritime theme. There are literally a hundred photos and paintings of sailing vessels on the walls, while the carpet features large medallions highlighted with an image of a three-masted schooner.

Built a hundred years ago as a home for the elderly, the Tudor House was taken over as a mess around the time of the First World War. It also served as living quarters for Navy personnel. But by 1937, the building got an honourable discharge and began civilian duty as a bar—a task it has faithfully accomplished ever since.

"This bar is unique in Victoria," proclaims Cheryl the DJ—and she ought to know, because she provides the musical heartbeat for one of the hottest dance floors in the city. "The Port-of-Call is a military bar," she emphasizes. "When the ships are in, the guys want rock 'n' roll . . . and while they're out and there's more women here then we play more rap." Although the place is good for a quiet dinner and a brew early in the evening, the large video screen looming over the dance floor will have everyone primed to boogie not long after the sun goes down. Weekends are the craziest, of course, but there's dancing here every night of the week. (A typed sheet of paper near the DJ cage lists their favourite dumb questions, including: "Got any STONES, man?"; "But it's popular in Ontario"; and the poignant, "If I give you a blank, will you tape it for me?")

If you take your dancing and drinking seriously, consider enlisting at the Port-of-Call!

Beer Trivia

fter Prohibition was repealed in 1921, the city of Victoria opted to tay dry (and remained so until 1953). Esquimalt, however, had ore than its share of beer parlours, and after closing time the ohnson Street Bridge became a conduit for dozens of soused atrons riding the buses back to town.

Pub Philosopher

No animal ever invented anything so bad as drunkenness — or so ood as drink."

— *G.K. Chesterton*

The Four Mile Roadhouse

199 Island Highway, Victoria
Telephone: 479-3346

Hours: 11:30 a.m. - 11:30 p.m., Monday - Thursday; 11:30 a.m. - midnight, Friday - Saturday; 11:30 a.m. - 11:00 p.m., Sunday

The Navigator: Follow Gorge Road all the way out, turn left at the Admirals Road T-junction, then take a right at the intersection where Craigflower becomes the old highway (just beside historic Craigflower Manor). The Four Mile is just ahead, on the left.

Many of the Island's pubs have a skeleton or so rattling in the closet, but only **The Four Mile Roadhouse** has a genuine ghost—an appropriate enough accessory, I suppose, for the fourth-oldest building still standing in Victoria. Dating originally from 1858, the Four Mile was renovated and made into a restaurant a decade ago by Graham and Linda Haymes, who won a restoration award from the Hallmark Society for their scrupulous efforts. In 1988 the pub was added, and it is indeed in the, umm, spirit of a gorgeous, nineteenth-century country roadhouse. Post and beam construction, oak flooring, antique furniture, Persian carpets and brass lamps create a mood of easy elegance, while pioneering knick-knacks such as ceramic bed warmers are dotted along the elaborate moulding near the ceiling. The main room boasts a seventeen-foot barrel vault ceiling, where your eye will be drawn first to the large fireplace and then to the beautiful stained glass window that surmounts it. This is a rendering of "the white lady," a long-ago relative of Four Mile House pioneer Peter Calvert. Her ghostly form was often seen looking out to sea nearby to where she was buried. But even though the white lady hasn't been spotted for decades now, the pub/restaurant has its own ghostly presence, a quiet fellow named Jake. This benign spectre occasionally appears in a small room, where he'll be spotted by a waitress out of the corner of her eye; yet when someone goes to take his order . . . he's gone!

Tough luck on old Jake—for the food here is truly excellent. The same kitchen that serves up gourmet vittles for the restaurant also services the pub, and the lucky patrons can dine light on humus and pita and calamari or go for heartier fare such as the teriyaki burger, the steak sandwich or the salmon filet. Service is prompt and friendly, and contributes to the cheery bustle that is the hallmark of this attractive establishment. Many people make a point of coming here on Wednesday and Thursday, for toe-tapping entertainment by some of the area's best pop and neo-folkie musicians. "This is definitely a View Royal pub," says Graham. "Because we're a bit out of the city you have to drive here, and it's mostly locals . . . they're a good bunch."

Even if you don't believe in ghosts, you'll have no trouble believing in the fine times and great food that are offered by the Four Mile Roadhouse, where Victoria's rich past can be savoured over a slow pint or two.

Beer Trivia

Despite some spirited competition from other beer-producing countries, the world leader is the United States, which generates nearly twenty billion litres per year.

Pub Philosopher

Better a bottle in front of me than a frontal lobotomy."

—Tom Waits

51

Six-Mile House

494 Island Highway, Victoria
Telephone: 478-3121

Hours: 11 a.m. - 1:30 a.m., Monday - Saturday; 11 a.m. - 11 p.m., Sunday

The Navigator: Take the Colwood Exit from the Island Highway and go west .5 km to Parsons Bridge and Six-Mile House, on the right.

Dating from the earliest days of Victoria history, **The Six-Mile House** was built in 1855 as Parsons Bridge Hotel. This rambling establishment quickly became a favourite haunt of British sailors, who came from the nearby Esquimalt naval base to slake their considerable thirst. By the 1880s the Parsons had become a "roadhouse," complete with the new "six-mile" name, marking it as an official drop-off along the stage coach route. In 1898 a fire devastated the original wooden building, and a Tudor-style carriage house arose in its place. The Six-Mile proudly lays claim to holding the province's longest-running pub licence.

Gorgeously restored in 1980, this patriarch of beer parlours became a. model for many of the neighbourhood pubs that followed. Brass rails, leaded glass windows, high ceilings, oak floors, Persian carpets, ornate Edwardian lamps and stained glass perfectly recreate a turn-of-the-century elegance. The giant brick fireplace boasts a tiny cannon on one side, while the other side displays a wooden bellows from the first blacksmith shop on Saltspring Island. Seating capacity exceeds 220, and there's a sequence of several rooms, each with its own mood. (Look for the coffered mahogany ceiling and the original Parsons Bridge Hotel sign, just to the left of the darts nook, behind the bar and past the wrought iron spiral staircase.) In a whimsical touch, few of the tables actually have life-size, five-globed lamp standards soaring out of their centre, while the all-tile bathrooms feature Pre-Raphaelite art on the walls. This isn't your typical beer parlour!

But possibly the Six-Mile's biggest influence came from the emphasis placed on its kitchen: this was the first pub in the area to make a convincing argument that you didn't have to go to a fancy restaurant to get a great meal. The big chalkboard near the ordering bar boasts a few dozen daily specials (chosen from a recipe repertoire exceeding 200), including regular fare such as prime rib, pizza and gourmet snacks like scallops wrapped in bacon. The accent is on fresh, seasonal ingredients—particularly local fish—and the results are consistently excellent meals: hefty portions at surprisingly reasonable prices.

Whether it's summer and you're drawn to the garden terrace with the gazebo and vine arbour, or those winter-time snows have you huddling up to the fireplace, the turn-of-the-century elegance and cheery atmosphere of this classic pub will dissolve your cares long before that first pint has been emptied.

Pub Philosopher

envy people who drink — at least they know what to blame everything on."
— Oscar Levant

Country Rose Pub

592 Ledsham Road, Colwood
Telephone: 478-4200

Hours: 11 a.m. - 11:30 p.m., Monday - Wednesday; 11 a.m. - midnight, Thursday; 11 a.m. - 12:30 a.m., Friday - Saturday; 11 a.m. - 11 p.m., Sunday

The Navigator: Take the Colwood Exit from the Island Highway and head through Colwood, past Royal Roads Military College. A few hundred metres later turn left onto Ledsham Road (which is bounded by Corona Foods on one side, a Dairy Queen on the other).

Sited in a heritage home dating from 1925, the **Country Rose Pub** is all the excuse anyone should need to pay a visit to Colwood. As the area's only neighbourhood pub, the Country Rose goes out of its way to offer the congeniality you'd expect from a visit with friends in the country.

Cosy comfort seems to have been the theme that inspired Dick and Judy Michaud when they lovingly created their pub conversion back in 1986. Upholstered antique wooden chairs are grouped around most tables, while some bench and bay window seating is available for those who really want to kick back and forget their troubles. The post and beam construction, panelled walls and tasteful millwork are a good example of period architecture—and clear evidence that "rustic" charms can be very refined indeed. A more contemporary mood is established on the pub's lower level where the sports TV, pool table and darts areas are warmed by freestanding "acorn" fireplace with a copper hood. On the upper level, a brick fireplace boasts a large wreath of dried flowers, while several attractive floral prints further promote the horticultural theme. Three stained glass windows and a pair of old-fashioned trays mounted on ceiling beams portray romantic images of the pub's namesake rose.

With all those flowers inside, it shouldn't be surprising that the

Country Rose's gardens are a quiet riot of floral extravagance. Although the pub always had fine gardens, they've latterly been taken over and radically improved by John Dronyk, a pensioner who retired out here from Ontario. John's dedication and imagination are such that the gardens are a must-see during the spring and summer. (Several brides have insisted that their wedding pictures be shot amidst these gorgeous blooms.)

The menu features standard pub fare, but with a real emphasis placed on quality. All the meals are made from scratch, there's no MSG, and fresh ingredients are a priority. Their fish and chips, always made with halibut and prepared with a tasty beer batter, are the specialty of the house. Some of the other menu highlights include the steak sandwich, the ribs and, for lighter eaters, the humus and pita and the deep-fried zucchini. Sunday brunchers with no fear of calories and cholesterol will want to treat themselves to the eggs benedict special.

With all the fine hiking and swimming and other outdoor opportunities available in the Colwood-Metchosin area, a post-recreation visit for refreshments and a bite to eat at this friendly pub is the perfect conclusion to any expedition. You don't have to be a horticulturist—or even a bride—to feel right at home in the Country Rose!

Island Trivia

The 1858 Gold Rush turned Victoria, a frontier town with a population of 600, into a real city. More than 25,000 miners passed through, and such was the frantic pace of business that 225 buildings were erected in one six-week period.

Seventeen-Mile House

5126 Sooke Road, Victoria
Telephone: 642-5942

Hours: 11:00 a.m. - midnight, Monday - Thursday;
11:00 a.m. - 1:00 a.m., Friday - Saturday; 11:30
a.m. - 8:00 p.m., Sunday

The Navigator: Follow the signs from the Island Highway
towards Colwood and Sooke. The Seventeen-Mile
House is right on Sooke Road, 12 km past the
highway exit.

Although Victoria and the Island don't lack for historic
roadhouses, it's pretty hard to top the funky charms o
Seventeen-Mile House. Built in the 1890s and known originally a:
the British Ensign, this hotel for sportsmen soon got its curren
name, which identified its place along the stagecoach route out t
Sooke. The hotel was also soon identified with a different spor
those who were unmarried—or, as was more often the case, marrie
to the wrong person—headed these ways to engage in som
passionate bump and tickle away from wagging tongues.

A beer licence was obtained in the post-Prohibition 1920s, and th
Seventeen-Mile became a mecca for thirsty drinkers for mile
around. "Ma" Wilson, the pub's most colourful owner, operated th
place from 1940 to 1970, and a celebrated thirty-year stint it was. A
autocratic moralist, Wilson would shut down the business during th
supper hour, and she never allowed family men to get their hands c
more than two beers. "Ma" also slept with a loaded shotgun und
the bed, and certainly had the respect of her numerous customers!

Today, the pub still has links with the past. Current owne
Bill and Chuck Wilson are grandsons of Mrs. Wilson, wh
installed the striking Italianate tiling that you notice when fir
entering the Seventeen-Mile. There are five different room
ranging from a pool nook to an intimate, elegantly wallpaper
room in the back that seems ideal for a romantic dinner.
150-year-old piano stands near the wood and brick bar; players a

welcome, but a sign asks you to be gentle. Old-timey photos on the wall are windows back to our not-so-distant frontier past: the picturesque rural setting, isolated in a forest of Douglas fir trees, makes it all the easier to imagine those rough and ready days when brawls and the occasional gunshot brought a lively pace to the activities at the Seventeen-Mile.

The only real change to this fine pub is the kitchen, which was added five years ago. The food is super, ranging from nachos and gourmet hot dogs to a clam feast or a hearty steak sandwich. The daily specials are well worth considering, too. This popular bar used to have a ghost, allegedly the spirit of an earlier owner who hanged himself, but his presence hasn't been felt since the mid-1980s. The most obvious explanation for the absent apparition comes when you investigate the pub's photo album: under the "Celebrities" section you'll see photos and autographs from those celebrated Ghostbusters Bill Murray and Dan Aykroyd, who chanced upon the pub in October of 1985 and spent a few delighted hours here.

"This is a great place to work," declares long-time waitress Janet Anthonie. "We get a really varied clientele, everybody from loggers to little old ladies who come here to sip their tea." She's even proud of their ball team, which is, she confesses, truly terrible. "We try to win the most sportsmanlike trophy," she laughs. "It's the only chance we've got."

Beer Trivia

on Solberg of Oslo, Norway has amassed 322,000 different beer labels from around the world.

The Loghouse Pub

2323 Millstream Road, Victoria
Telephone: 474-1989

Hours: 11:30 a.m. - 11:30 p.m., Monday - Thursday;
11:30 a.m. - 12:30 a.m., Friday - Saturday; 11:30
a.m. - 10:30 p.m., Sunday

The Navigator: Heading up the Island Highway, turn right onto
Millstream Road. Pub is just a few hundred
metres along, on the right.

Truly unique pubs seem to be the product of an extra dollop of
love, care and imagination, and such is surely the case with **The
Loghouse**, a tasteful and charming tribute to the pioneering spirit
that still lingers on at the edges of the Western Communities.
Comprising two main rooms, this 4,000-square-foot beauty took
more than a year to plan and ten months to build, opening on July
15, 1988. Made entirely of logs—except for the tile roof—this is an
establishment made to the theme of "country comfort." It is
decorated with a profusion of homesteading gear, including a great
collection of vintage kerosene lamps, a wooden-toothed rake,
old-fashioned bottles, first-generation logging gear, and an antique
woven creel box with fishing pole to match. A collection of
great-grandma's kitchen gear is arrayed above where you place your
food orders, while the well-stoked fireplace offers a timeless
solution to the problem of winter chills. Some of the more modern
touches include a specially woven wool carpet patterned with fir
trees, and a sequence of stained glass panels above the bar depicting
a colourful frieze of bottles. This is one place that will coax even
the most frantic businessman to slow down and try the pleasures of
life in the rustic lane!

Exuding a natural warmth because of its honey-coloured wood
walls—the logs were stripped of their bark with power hoses to
eliminate any scarring—The Loghouse emphasizes old-fashioned
ways to pass the time. A large library of books, magazines and
newspapers is provided for the solitary browser, while two large

tables provide dozens of games to while away an evening (several of the tables are actually game boards, inlaid with everything from backgammon to Trivial Pursuit patterns). "We encourage a friendly, family living room atmosphere," explains Lorraine Langlois, who, along with husband Paul, owns the pub. "Our customers know that they can amuse their friends here without any loud or forced entertainment."

In fact, the only thing loud here is the praise for the kitchen, which prepares all its food on the premises, from exclusively premium ingredients (for example, their popular fish and chips are made with halibut, and the chips are deep-fried in peanut oil). Friday and Saturday nights feature the roast beef dinner, starring softball-sized Yorkshire puddings. Lunchtimes favour a lot of pasta dishes and other specials, while the core menu always has the hefty "logger" burger and tasty "knotchos."

And now that the "settling in" process has just finished (as the logs dried, the walls have gradually shrunk five inches, necessitating an incremental lowering of the roof via screw jacks in the uprights), The Loghouse can relax even more. For even though this grand pub was built on the former site of a tourist-trap ghost town, the only spirit in evidence these days (other than the ones behind the bar) is a pervasive sense of cosy contentment.

Beer Trivia

The world's largest bottle is just under seven feet tall, and has a circumference greater than five feet. It was displayed at Australia's Laidley Tourist Festival, where it was filled with 418 litres of Laidley Gold, a unique wheat beer.

Pub Philosopher

"Prohibition makes you want to cry into your beer, and denies you the beer to cry into."

— *Don Marquis*

59

Ma Miller's

Goldstream Inn
2903 Sooke Lake Road, Victoria
Telephone: 478-3512

Hours: 11:00 a.m. - 1:00 a.m., Monday - Saturday; 11:00 a.m. - midnight, Sunday

The Navigator: Follow the Island Highway out of Victoria. A short distance before Goldstream, turn left onto Sooke Lake Road (opposite the Shell gas station). Pub is a half-mile up on the left.

For a real taste of Victoria's frontier past, you should hoist a glass or two at **Ma Miller's Goldstream Inn**, which has been in business since 1864. Built on the site of the historic Goldstream Hotel, which served as a much-needed stopover on the painfully rutted wagon road that connected Victoria and Cowichan, Ma Miller's is in its third incarnation. (It was destroyed by fire in 1873, and again in 1923.)

Although the Inn had been run by the widowed Mary Miller since 1915, it wasn't until 1931 that she overcame opposition from the Prohibition League and received official permission to open up a beer parlour. During her subsequent fifteen-year tenure, "Ma" ran the joint like a despot: all the local miners, loggers and other working-class drinkers were kept firmly in line by her iron rule. When she retired in 1946, beer cost but ten cents! She died twenty years later, at age ninety, and the Goldstream Inn then became known as "Ma Miller's" to honour this feisty woman.

The pub was completely renovated in the spring of 1985, and the tasteful decor is true Tudor: leaded windows, wood flooring, stained glass, wallpaper and ceiling fans. The right-hand side of the pub is dominated by a handsome fieldstone fireplace, complete with a large hand-carved wood mantle that combines elements of Art Nouveau and Canadiana. On the adjoining wall hangs a giant oil painting of the Goldstream Inn in bygone days; a horse and carriage are drawn up outside, and a British Ensign is snapping in the breeze.

A nearby oak bookcase acts as a room divider, further separating this more intimate space from the central portion of the pub.

Ma Miller's enthusiastically caters to the locals, creating a natural entertainment focus for that fast-growing neighbourhood. There's singalong karaoke on Tuesdays, with an accent on the hurt and heartbreak of country music. Electronic trivia takes the stage on Wednesdays, and there's a pool tournament every Thursday ($3.50 admission). The pub also sponsors an annual fishing derby.

One of Ma Miller's major drawing cards is the fine kitchen, which offers generous portions at fair prices. Whether you go for the fish and chips, the Caesar salad, the chicken fingers or one of the burgers, you'll find that the fare is tasty indeed.

Even though "Ma" is no longer on hand to keep everyone in line, her spirit seems to linger on in the homey and attractive atmosphere of the pub that bears her name.

Beer Trivia

Beer has always been serious, state-controlled business. In ancient Babylon, any irregularities in the sale of beer merited the death penalty. In thirteenth-century England, rules were only slightly less harsh. Those who evaded the beer tax had their right hands lopped off, their houses destroyed, and suffered five-year banishments.

Duncan and Area

~

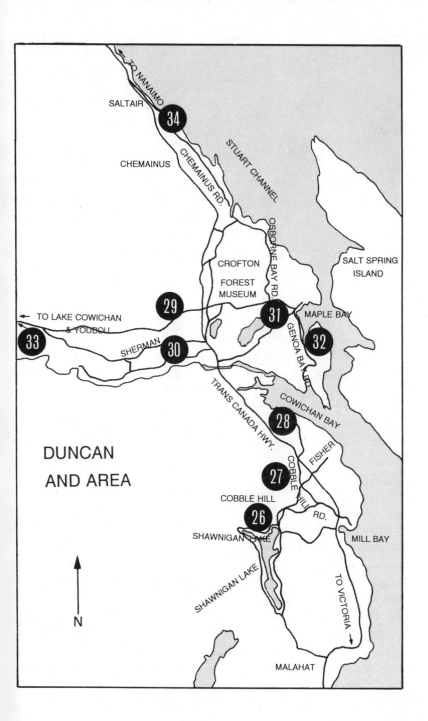

DUNCAN
AND AREA

N

The Black Swan

2809 Shawnigan Lake Road, Cobble Hill
Telephone: 743-5133

Hours: 11 a.m. - midnight, Sunday - Thursday; 11 a.m. -
1 a.m., Friday - Saturday

The Navigator: Heading up the Malahat, take the South Shawnigan
turnoff and follow the East Shawnigan Lake Road
to Shawnigan Village; go through the four-way
stop and when the road forms a Y, turn right onto
Shawnigan Lake Road. Pub is 400 metres up,
on the left.

Although Shawnigan Lake isn't the most logical spot to go
looking for an urbanely uptown pub, **The Black Swan** more than
lives up to its name. Boasting elegant millwork, split levels, burled
tables and comfy furniture, this attractively scaled drinking
establishment has a contemporary flair that has earned the loyalty of
a youngish, high-energy crowd. Although it has been around for a
few decades, part of the original bar has been transformed into an
adjacent beer and wine store. The renovations/additions include a
handsome raised nook, which has a stone fireplace that has
inspired many a cheerful conversation during the rainy months.
(And aside from the framed print of a mascot swan, there is a
sequence of rugged logging photos that keep the place from
becoming too hoighty-toighty.)

Don't get distracted by the ultra-colourful Wurlitzer jukebox
in the middle of the pub—sure it looks spiffy, but it's only a
reproduction. Right next to it is the real goods, a 1910 Shell service
station gas pump that's been converted into a fish tank. It's a
souvenir from owner Jack Rosendaal, who used to pump gas at the
nearby Shawnigan Garage till he wiped the oil off his hands for the
last time and started pumping beer instead.

The Black Swan tends to fill up with locals, particularly during
the off-season, but some regulars head in from as far away as Nanaimo
and Victoria. (And one of the friendliest habitues is Buddy, an old

black dog who brings his owner out for a drink most evenings. The more it looks like you're going to give Buddy a pat, the faster his tail wags!) Monday night belongs to the dart devotees, and every second weekend there's dancing to live music, everything from rock to country. The mantles are jammed with trophies, and while a few of them are from the curling and baseball teams that Jack sponsors, most of the trophies are prized souvenirs of the pub's own Swan Days, the highlight of which is an inner tube race down Shawnigan Creek. The festivities include a beer garden and dance, and are scheduled for the first weekend in August.

"We're known for our burgers here," says the waitress proudly as she drops off a couple of frosty glasses. But you only need an appetite for good times and the chance to meet some new friends if you glide off in search of the Black Swan.

Beer Trivia

Black Velvet, a mix of champagne and stout, was allegedly fashioned to commemorate the death of Prince Albert, husband of Queen Victoria.

Pub Philosopher

"The tavern chair is the throne of human felicity."

— *Samuel Johnson*

The Cobblestone Inn

3566 Hollan Road, Mill Bay
Telephone: 743-4232

Hours: 11 a.m. - midnight, daily

The Navigator: Heading up the Island Highway, two miles past Mill Bay, look for the new set of traffic lights and turn left onto Hutchinson, followed by a right onto Watson, a left onto Fisher, and a quick right onto Hollan.

Friendly and unpretentious—imagine a large rec room that's been lavished with attention and transformed into a Tudor pub—**The Cobblestone Inn** has been offering homestyle cooking and a cosy social centre for the locals of Shawnigan and Cobble Hill for almost a decade now. With half-timbered construction, art nouveau Tiffany lamps, a collection of international beer coasters, and a row of antiques running high along one wall, this authentic neighbourhood pub offers a heartfelt invitation to leave your cares at the door and enjoy some countrified comfort and hospitality. A stuffed pheasant hides in one corner, while a fox seems poised for flight on the mantle over the brick fireplace: just a few reminders of the charming rural heritage that has persuaded the locals to stay put, out of the orbit of the hustle-bustle cities nearby.

They are justly proud of the Cobblestone's kitchen, and the ordering gets done up at the big counter near the door. There's no fixed menu—"We cook as we go," says manager Sharon Lee—and the numerous daily specials are colourfully written on the big menu board. Depending on what's fresh and available, you could be choosing from various seafood dishes, pepper steak, cajun chicken and old standbys such as hamburgers and halibut and chips. Lighter eaters can order from the appetizer menu (the calamari, cooked with dill and lots of sweet onion, are super).

Owner Bud Lee, who also operates a family restaurant in Duncan, makes sure that the regulars think of the Cobblestone as "their" place. The pub sponsors baseball and curling teams, and is actively involved in the darts scene: Mondays and Thursdays their teams compete with legions and other pubs. There's live music on the weekends, and do-it-yourselfers get a go on Tuesdays, when karaoke allows amateur singers the chance to vocalize to their favourite top-forty tunes. Summertime offers its own particular pleasures, when the outdoor patio allows patrons the opportunity to savour an *al fresco* ale.

Next time you're cruising up the Malahat, or have spent the day swimming or water-skiing at Shawnigan Lake, do what the locals do and take that hearty appetite to the Cobblestone Inn.

Beer Trivia

Among the practical, hard-drinking Norse folk, their important meetings were known as "ales" due to the fact that a drink of ale after completing a contract was thought to make it legally binding. Such contracts were so common that the expression "beer house testimony" eventually became an accepted legal term to the Norse.

Al Capone is estimated to have grossed up to $100 million per year from his bootlegging operations.

The Windjammer

1695 Cowichan Bay Road, Cowichan Bay
Telephone: 746-9027

Hours: Monday - Thursday, 11 a.m. - midnight; Friday -
                     Saturday, 11 a.m. - 1 a.m.

The Navigator: Seven km past Mill Bay, turn right on Cowichan
                     Bay Road, continuing for another 4 km (the
                     Windjammer is at the bottom of a long hill, on
                     the right).

Right in the middle of some of the best bicycling on
Vancouver Island sits **The Windjammer**, an oasis of refreshing
beer and nourishing food (actually, if you don't feel like going
for a spin on your new mountain bike, you can just leave it in the
garage, as most of the clientele comes by car and boat). Set in the
charming seaside hamlet of Cowichan Bay, a picturesque
sequence of quaint houses and shops dotted along the curving
shoreline, this friendly pub will reward anyone's visit. If you're
clever enough to arrive in the heat of summer, make a dash for an
umbrella-topped table out on the harbourside balcony: gentle sea
breezes waft by as you get a seagull's-eye view of the numerous
pleasure boats bobbing at the government wharf. Dominating the
horizon is green and hilly Mount Tsouhalem, which rises above
nearby Genoa Bay to a considerable height. But during August
you may get distracted from that postcard view if the killer
whales come chasing into the bay in pursuit of the salmon that
are returning to spawn up the Cowichan River.

"We sell a lot of food here," declares owner John Shumka,
and it's not idle boasting. The kitchen is the heart of any genuine
pub, and the Windjammer is no exception. Although the cheese
burger is the best seller, a lot of patrons insist that the baron of
beef is the real star on the menu (both of these beauties are
homemade, and they're big). And after a fine meal, those
seeking some food for thought can amble down the street to
the Maritime Museum, which offers an attractive seafaring history

of the area (located in the Cowichan Bay Maritime Centre, along the strip just before the Bluenose Cafe).

Whether you're seeking an ice-cold Corona, a hearty steak sandwich or maybe some high-spirited dancing to a pop-rock trio on Friday night, The Windjammer makes for an excellent port of call.

Beer Trivia

The word "tumbler" derives from the round-bottomed glasses that were cunningly designed not to be put down until you had emptied your glass.

Pub Philosopher

"Brandy, n. A cordial composed of one part thunder-and-lightning, one part remorse, two parts bloody murder, one part death-hell-and-the-grave, and four parts clarified Satan. Dose: a headful all the time."

*— Ambrose Bierce (*The Devil's Dictionary*)*

C.V. Station

Cowichan Valley Inn
6457 Norcross Road, Duncan
Telephone: 748-2722

Hours: 11:30 a.m. - 1:30 a.m., Monday - Saturday; 11:30 a.m. - 11 p.m., Sunday

The Navigator: On the left of the Island Highway just north of Duncan (directly over from the Forest Museum).

The old steam train patiently standing guard at the Forest Museum just north of Duncan has long been a familiar sight to Island Highway travellers. Although its primary purpose is to draw attention to a fine assemblage of historic forestry machinery, it seems fitting that this locomotive landmark is also a reference point for **The C.V. Station,** a railway-themed pub located directly across the highway at the Cowichan Valley Inn.

Although its red, railway-station facade creates the feeling that The C.V. Station is part of this country's (sadly dwindling) rail service, the "passengers" who board here have no destination in mind other than the good times and fine food that have been attracting business for nearly a decade now.

The railway theme is deftly continued inside, culminating with the bar, whose varnished woods, brass elbow rail and pair of strategically placed signalman's lamps capture the spirit of a railway club car. Elsewhere, a handsome array of brass rails, moss-green walls, stained glass, old-fashioned lamps and fans, and elegantly milled dark woods evoke the plush comforts of the Edwardian era. (And don't leave without inspecting all the archival photos, dotted along the walls, which recall the glory days of the E & N Railway.)

Adding some contemporary comfort—and more than a few calories—is one of the most upscale kitchens on the Island's pubbing circuit. While the lunch menu has some pretty ambitious items, including French onion soup, quiche lorraine and frittatas (and don't overlook the always-popular Caesar salad and cheese toast combo), dinnertime is like a visit to a three-star restaurant.

Escargot, oysters Rockefeller, prawn brochettes, medallions of pork, bouillabaisse and five different pastas are but a few of the offerings.

And while trying to walk off that slab of Black Forest cake you gobbled for dessert, take a peek at the Inn's big draw, a life-size wood carving of a fierce grizzly bear and her two cubs, posed on the grass overlooking the highway. (Chainsaw carver Terry McKinnon made more than 25,000 cuts to create this vivid tableau.)

Whether you're in need of a fine meal or a refreshingly crisp beer, the unique club car comfort of The C.V. Station is just the ticket. All aboard!

Beer Trivia

The Germans pioneered the use of hops to flavour beer. And because hops also act as a preservative, this meant that German beer was the first that could be exported.

The Oak and Carriage

3287 Cowichan Lake Road, Duncan
Telephone: 746-4144

Hours: 11 a.m. - midnight, Sunday - Thursday; 11 a.m. - 1 a.m., Friday - Saturday

The Navigator: From the Island Highway, take the first left north of McDonald's (just past the Tourist Information Centre), and then an immediate right onto Sherman Road. Go 1 km to first stop sign, turn left and the pub is on the left.

The chances are good that if you're in a bar with a sign saying "Ring the bell and buy a round for the house," then you are most likely in a *real* neighbourhood pub. Such is certainly the case with **The Oak and Carriage**, a cosy Tudor-style establishment that takes sufficient time off from all the carousing and camaraderie to support about half the athletic activities in all of Duncan (the glittering trophies on the wall and mantle reflect their support of soccer, rugby, football, golf, baseball, hockey, volleyball and—of course—darts). That support is happily reciprocated by many of Duncan's pubbing patrons, who seek out the comfy chairs here to celebrate the latest sporting triumph . . . or else commiserate with each other in the despond of defeat.

"There's about eighty percent locals who come here," estimates genial owner Bob McDonald, who, along with wife Stephanie, has run the place since it first opened in 1980. "It's a real family environment!" Bob seems to be a born publican—for part-time work he bought the faltering Saltair Pub in Chemainus and handily revived it before selling it—and his Oak and Carriage offers first-class comfort and service. The set-up is "olde English," with an oak-beamed central room dominated by the bar and a manor-sized brick fireplace. China plates, horse brasses and old-fashioned prints set an eighteenth-century mood (the washrooms are identified as "Lords" and "Ladys"). A couple of nooks provide the opportunity for more intimate sipping, while many patrons seek out the alcove seating built into the bay windows, which spill a soft light into the pub.

With dinner-time lineups and a regular takeout business, the food quality at the Oak and Carriage speaks for itself. There is no set menu, but a wide selection of ever-changing daily specials is listed on the board near the bar. "If you want it, I'll cook it," declares chef Giorgio, who insists on using the freshest possible ingredients. Selections can range from fish and chips and New York steak to savoury Italian dishes and prawns sizzled in a generous splash of Pernod. And with prices pegged on the moderate side, it's no wonder that fewer Duncan folk are cooking all their dinners at home.

There's always a convivial atmosphere here, with occasional live music and an old upright piano that gets played on an ad hoc basis when a patron wants to share a tune or two. Mondays are dart nights, and even though Giorgio speaks of Bob's prowess at this sport in a hushed voice, the cheery owner quickly puts his own athletic ability into perspective. "I'm really not a very good dart player . . . the only person I can beat is Giorgio," he laughs.

So, if you're looking for a cosy spot to quaff an ale—and maybe want to try your luck at the dart board—then roll on up to the ever-friendly Oak and Carriage.

Island Trivia

Victoria's unreliable coal gas streetlights quickly gave way to electricity; by 1889, there were seventy-nine such street lamps distributed throughout the city. But very few houses had electricity before the First World War.

The Brigantine Inn

6777 Beaumont Avenue, Maple Bay
Telephone: 746-5422

Hours:	Sunday - Thursday, 11 a.m. - midnight; Friday - Saturday, 11 a.m. - 1 a.m.
The Navigator	Follow the signs east from Duncan to Maple Bay. The Brigantine is located on the waterfront just beyond the government dock.

Few pubs *anywhere* can claim a view to rival that possessed by **The Brigantine Inn**: newcomers should definitely grab their glasses and head out to the 500-square-foot deck overlooking the water to best, umm, drink in that stunning panorama of Maple Bay and Sansum Narrows, with Saltspring Island's Baynes Peak soaring in the background. Summer or winter, rain or shine, this view alone more than justifies an expedition out to The Brigantine.

But this fine pub has many more charms than just its view. Dominating the interior is a ship-shaped bar, complete with spars and rigging. Adding to the atmosphere is the pub's sturdy furniture—hefty wooden chairs finished in cowhide, tables sturdy enough for swashbucklers to duel on—that was hand-crafted by a Scandinavian artisan in Horseshoe Bay on the Mainland. As well, there are summer barbecues out on the deck, and a dock has just been installed so that boaters can come in directly.

The Brigantine has only been around since 1979, yet it's carrying on a century-old pubbing tradition: the Maple Bay Inn had a liquor licence for many decades, till it burned down in the late 1970s. And owner Brian Hebbert, a Maple Bay man from way back has had family living in the area since 1887. It should be no surprise, then, that Brian runs his pub with friendly, old-fashioned flair. Even the newest arrivals feel at home right away, while the regulars are always ready to help celebrate with a range of special events, including an anniversary party on June 1, carol singing just before Christmas and a New Year's Eve party that keeps all the participants awash in good cheer and good times.

Even though the kitchen at The Brigantine serves up a full menu of hearty pub fare, this cheery pub is also cherished for the musical good times that are offered. Aside from the Sunday night jam, which features audience participation (and occasional drop-in guests like Willie P. Bennett and Diamond Joe White), they also book a name-brand band such as the Shuffle Demons or the Persuaders every three weeks or so. So, for food, fun and that incredible view, don't pass up a visit to the Brigantine Inn.

Beer Trivia

The largest collection of beer cans — nearly 15,000 — is owned by John F. Ahrens of Mount Laurel, New Jersey. (And he's not the only weirdo: a collector paid $6,000 for a Rosalie Pilsner can in 1981!)

Pub Philosopher

'Alcohol is a very necessary article . . . . It enables Parliament to do things at eleven at night that no sane person would do at eleven in the morning."

— George Bernard Shaw

The Shipyard Marine Pub

Maple Bay Marina
6145 Genoa Bay Road, Maple Bay
Telephone: 746-8482

Hours: 11:00 a.m. - midnight, daily; (4 p.m. - midnight
during non-summer months)

The Navigator: Follow signs from Duncan towards Maple Bay,
then turn right on Genoa Bay Road. The
Shipyard is 3 km along, at the Maple Bay Marina
(look for the Mai-Tai Dining Lounge sign).

The Island's more senior pubcrawlers will remember the
Wheelhouse Marine Pub at Maple Bay Marina. Well, that
establishment was recently jettisoned from the fleet when the
marina's four new owners—corporately known as Maple Bay
Resorts—designed and constructed the nearby **Shipyard Marine
Pub** as part of their marina enhancement. Because it was converted
from a working shipyard, this unique pub comes by its nautical
themes with impeccable credentials. The two-storey interior, which
gives the effect of a giant boat flipped over on its gunwales, is
decorated with Japanese glass floats and brass boating lamps. A
moss-green dinghy hangs on chains from the ceiling, while the
tables all have inset, glass-covered ovals containing antique maps.
The marina side of the pub is all window, with the exposed
rope-wound framing suggesting the ribs of a boat.

But The Shipyard, bright and airy, is anything but a nautical
museum. Blond wood, lots of plants and a tracery of orange and
green neon tubes add some downtown bistro flair to what could
easily be the most up-and-coming marine pub on the entire Island.
(Development plans for the marina include condos and a hotel.)

Maple Bay is the largest marina on Vancouver Island, and
during the prime boating season its 375 slips are booked solid by
both locals and tourists, eager to tie up at the beautiful and protected
Bird's Eye Cove. "We get a lot of boats from Seattle and also
California," explains co-owner Duane McLeod. "We even ge

vessels from New Zealand and Australia, because this is a good stopover en route to Alaska." But you don't have to know a lanyard from a lamprey to be made welcome at this pub, which draws land-loving regulars from a twenty-mile radius.

Duane and his fellow owners are proud of this establishment, and take pride in offering their customers the best in food, service and comfort. The fare includes all the pub classics such as fish and chips, steak sandwich and nachos, while their excellent clam chowder ably represents the marine influence. A lot of people also come crowding in for the live music on the weekends, which includes a dial-hopping mix of country, blues and soft rock.

And if the window wall doesn't give you a sufficient feel for the bustle on the docks, then grab your pint and move to the twenty-by forty-foot outdoor deck, which overlooks the entire marina and has been glassed in to keep out the wind.

There can be little doubt that for many West Coasters, the boating life is the ticket to happiness . . . and at Bird's Eye Cove, it's easy to understand why. You're not likely to forget those special moments, savouring a beer while the summer sunset casts its fleeting splash of colour on this sheltered bay. And if you can't enjoy that moment on the afterdeck of your own yacht, you're always welcome aboard The Shipyard!

Beer Trivia

s early as A.D. 616, Britain had laws governing the operation of
le houses.

The Lakeview

10524 North Shore Road, Youbou
Telephone: 745-6244

Hours: 11 a.m. - midnight, Sunday - Thursday; 11 a.m. - 1 a.m., Friday - Saturday

The Navigator: Follow the signs west from turnoff just north of Duncan. Once in Youbou, stay on the main drag and look for the distinctive, lantern-shaped sign in the parking lot.

For thirteen years **The Lakeview** has been providing a cosy social forum for the laid-back residents of the small Island community of Youbou. The current owners are Bill Belton and Betty Ronningen, and they are happily continuing that tradition of friendly and relaxed hospitality.

The pub itself boasts casual rustic comfort, including knotty-pine walls and cloth-covered swag lamps hanging from the ceiling. As befits an intimate, small-town pub, the emphasis is on providing a place where the locals can relax, enjoy themselves . . . and maybe complain about the latest provincial and federal political scandals. Few people complain, though, about the view from the outdoor deck, which offers attractive views of Lake Cowichan, home to some of the Island's best fishing. During the dog days of summer, a breeze often wafts off the lake and helps keep the deckside patrons cool as they quaff their ale and watch the hopeful fisherfolk trolling or casting for the rainbow trout that flash through the depths in considerable numbers.

Every neighbourhood pub has to have a kitchen, and The Lakeview just happens to adjoin the popular Lakeview Cafe. The full-service menu, available till 8 p.m., includes everything from soups, salads and chicken fingers to such hearty fare as steaks, pork chops and baron of beef. This is a friendly pub, and it's almost always relaxed . . . except on the weekends, when they bring in live country & western music and get the joint jumping to everything from cover versions of Willie Nelson songs to the occasional session of bluegrass picking (and don't pass up the Sunday evening jam sessions, when the more spirited locals entertain themselves).

A lot of tourists make their way here during the hot months, but by October The Lakeview's clientele will, with the exception of the occasional hunter stalking through, be mostly locals out to share in some community spirit. But whether you're the mayor of Youbou or an out-of-towner with a thirst for beer and good times, you're *always* made welcome at this friendly pub.

Beer Trivia

Much of the brewing done in Europe's medieval period was done in the local monasteries. The symbol "x," denoting the purity and strength of alcohol, originated with the monasteries; initially, though, the symbol was a crucifix.

Pub Philosopher

"Oh many a peer of England brews
Livelier liquor than the Muse
And malt does more than Milton can
To justify God's ways to man."

— *A.E. Houseman*

The Saltair

10519 Knight Road, Chemainus
Telephone: 246-4481

Hours: 11 a.m. - midnight, daily

The Navigator: From the south, turn right at the lights just past
the Fuller Lake Arena; go left at stop sign at golf
course. Three km along Old Chemainus Road,
turn right onto Knight (look for sign). From the
north, turn left off Island Highway onto
Chemainus Road opposite Coronation Square
Shopping Centre. Go 5.5 km to Knight Road
turn left.

Although we strongly believe that nothing should come
between a beer lover and his favourite potion, first-timers to **The
Saltair** should definitely postpone their pleasures till they've had
a cruise through nearby Chemainus, "the little town that did." Mill
closures in the early 1980s were turning this proud community into
a ghost town ... till some enterprising artists grabbed their
paintbrushes and started covering whole sides of buildings with
colourful murals depicting the town's economic and cultural history.
Now, no visit to Vancouver Island is complete without a visit to
Chemainus; and no visit to Chemainus is complete without a pint at
the Saltair!

This cosy pub has its own sense of history, being situated on
the ten-acre Knight homestead, which was for many years a tulip
field. The tulips are long gone, and the two ball fields that replaced
them have themselves become overgrown memories: the boys of
summer had to pack it in several seasons ago because of complaints
from the neighbours. (These days, The Saltair contents itself with
sponsoring a team in the local hockey league, and having euchre on
Tuesday evenings.) The trout pond is still there, however, and the
horseshoe pitch makes for great summer fun.

The turn-of-the-century Knight farmhouse, tastefully renovated
with wood panelling, a stone fireplace, Edwardian fans and lamps

and wood and leather chairs, offers old-fashioned comfort that feels just like home. A glassed-in sunroom at the back offers meadow views and the chance of seeing some local wildlife (or maybe you'll be busy playing an after-lunch game of crib or chess).

Hosts Bruce and Connie McQuade are proud to run a community-oriented pub, one that offers a friendly atmosphere, fine food, and live entertainment most weekends (ranging from local blues and country duos to recording stars like Diamond Joe White). Of particular merit is the kitchen, which provides an upscale mix of pub cuisine and more ambitious fare. At lunch you can choose among soups, salads, beef dip, pot pies and meatloaf. Dinnertime ups the calorie ante with their always-popular barbecued ribs, steak, curried chicken, tortellini and vegetarian lasagna. A lot of locals appear for the roast beef special on Fridays, while others angle for the famous homegrown trout.

With twenty years' experience at seeing to the needs of pub patrons, The Saltair Neighbourhood Pub has raised down-home hospitality to a high level. Add in that park-like setting, the relaxing ambience and the fine food, and you have the perfect excuse to go pubbing!

Pub Philosopher

One more drink and I'll be under the host."

— *Dorothy Parker, quoted at a party*

81

Quinn's Pub

Thetis Island Resort, Telegraph Harbour, Thetis Island
Telephone: 246-3464

Hours: 8 a.m. - midnight, daily; (From December to
                     April, closed Mondays)

The Navigator: The Pub is an 8-minute stroll up from the ferry
                     dock at Telegraph Harbour (turn right from the slip,
                     then turn left down Harbour Road). The ferry from
                     Chemainus takes about 25 minutes (but be sure to
                     check the schedule as some of the runs aren't direct
                     and will take longer). If arriving by boat, you can
                     find the pub at the first marina as you enter
                     Telegraph Harbour—look for the Esso sign.

Visitors to Chemainus should certainly book an hour to poke
around this fascinating hamlet, which was faced with ruin when the
mill shut down in the early 1980s. Then a bunch of artists grabbed
their brushes and began painting splendid murals on the sides of
many buildings; the result is one of the Island's biggest tourist
attractions, and a revived Chemainus became known as "the little
town that did." And when all that cultural activity gives you a thirst
hop the tugboat-sized ferry over to nearby Thetis Island and visit
Quinn's Pub, one of the friendliest havens on all of Vancouver Island.

A scant twenty-five-minute ferry ride from Chemainus, Thetis
Island is small and largely unspoiled: the year-round population is
just 250, rising to 450 when the summer seasonals drift over with
their fishing rods and suntan lotion. But you don't have to be
local—or even one of the thousands of annual boaters—to be made
welcome at the island's marine pub. Sited on handsome Telegraph
Harbour, Quinn's is an eminently casual place that overlooks a
fifty-berth marina (but during the crazy days of summer, as many as
120 boats will be rafted onto each other as the area throngs with
yachters looking for the good times that Quinn's is justly famous for).

Inside, the place is decidedly informal: wood and plaster walls
a slant roof and a ledge crowded with token memorabilia such as

old bottles, brass lamps, beer steins and even an antique typewriter. Chances are you won't be there long before you meet affable owner Peter Quinn, who's been in the hospitality business for two decades and has run his namesake pub for the last six years. "This is a *friendly* place," he insists, and he's got the facts to back it up. "During the summer, when we've got live music, the outdoor deck is just shakin' from all the dancers," he says. "I won't even let the waitresses out there after 10 p.m.—the guys will steal the beer right off the trays!"

Boaters come in from Vancouver, Seattle, even California, and the place has seen its share of celebrities, including Tom Selleck and "cowpunk" superstar k.d. lang. "She was here a couple of times," says Peter. "And next time she said she was going to join in on one of our jam sessions." Occasionally the rowdier tunes get put on the back burner while the owner indulges his interest in chamber music. The kitchen does its share to keep everyone happy as well, dishing up everything from fish and chips to oysters Rockefeller and chicken cordon bleu (serious carnivores should note the prime rib special on Saturday nights). And Peter is particularly proud of their annual Tricia Hunter fundraiser, run the third weekend in September. It's a real beer festival, complete with a side-of-beef barbecue, and the several thousand dollars they raise goes to help pay for a local girl who needs years of reconstructive facial surgery.

During the quieter times at Quinn's you can trade quips with the owner ("I tell 200 jokes a night") or admire the view of fir-clad Kuper Island across the narrow channel as you play darts on the outdoor deck. But when dance fever takes hold, it's every partyer for his or herself!

Beer Trivia

a 1575 banquet for Elizabeth I, her thirsty guests guzzled an tonishing 23,000 gallons of beer.

83

Nanaimo and Area

~

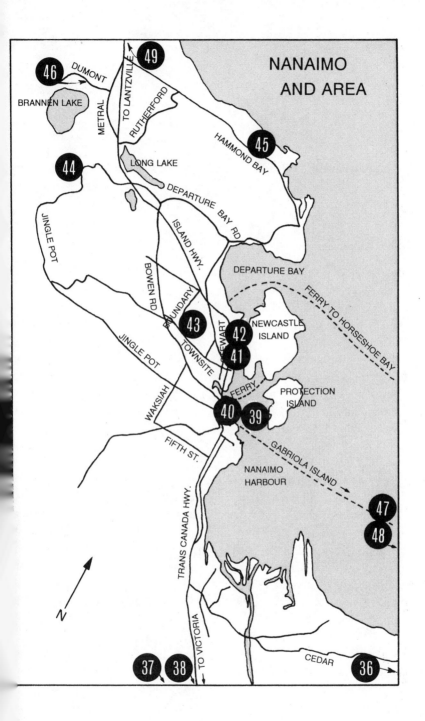

NANAIMO
AND AREA

46 DUMONT
BRANNEN LAKE

49 TO LANTZVILLE
METRAL
RUTHERFORD

45 HAMMOND BAY

44

LONG LAKE

DEPARTURE BAY RD.

JINGLE POT

ISLAND HWY.

BOWEN RD.

BOUNDARY

DEPARTURE BAY

FERRY TO HORSESHOE BAY

43 NEWCASTLE ISLAND

STEWART

42

41

TOWNSITE

JINGLE POT

WAKSIAH

FERRY

40 39

PROTECTION ISLAND

FIFTH ST.

GABRIOLA ISLAND

NANAIMO HARBOUR

47

48

TRANS CANADA HWY.

N

37 38

TO VICTORIA

CEDAR

36

85

Crow & Gate

2313 Yellow Point Road, Nanaimo
Telephone: 722-3731

Hours: 11 a.m. - 11 p.m., Monday - Thursday; 11 a.m. -
                     midnight, Friday - Saturday

The Navigator: Heading north of Cassidy on the Island Highway,
                     turn right on Cedar Road, keep going onto
                     Yellow Point Road, then 1 mile to the pub (it's
                     well signed).

Although the jousting and jesters of the Medieval Faire haven't
been seen since the mid-1980s, a visit to **The Crow & Gate** is still
like a visit to the Britain of long ago. A cheery "hello!" from the
publican greets all guests, who usually don't get around to ordering
from the bar until they've had a long, appreciative look at this
wonderful pub. With its hand-adzed beams, leaded glass, oriental
carpets, wooden tables and carved wooden chairs, decorative plates
hung on the walls and a brick fireplace large enough to roast a
sheep, the Tudor-styled Crow & Gate is like a hymn of praise to
Merry Olde England.

Built out in the middle of farm fields in 1972, this fine
establishment has the oldest neighbourhood pub licence in the
province. The current owners are the two Olson brothers and their
wives: Paul and Lianna and Bryce and Linda. They live on the
ten-acre farm that The Crow & Gate sits on, and they run the place
as a true family operation—one that caters to the locals with
assiduous care. "It's the people who live around here that really run
this place," declares Paul with a grin. "It's like we're just the
caretakers." He points to a row of character mugs hanging above the
bar: "Those are all owned by the regulars . . . it's nice for them to be
able to drink out of their own glass."

The food is legendary here, and if you want to be sure of having
a seat for dinner, you'd better make a reservation. Wednesday and
Saturday are traditional roast beef and Yorkshire pudding nights, while
the regular menu contains other classics, such as roast Cornish game

86

...en and shepherd's pie. Lunch is standard English pub fare, and ...nacks are available throughout the day. This is the area's most ...eliable social centre, whether you've dropped in for the dart ...ourney on Tuesday night, bridge the following evening, or just ...appen to be quaffing a pint when a fellow guest starts picking out ...ome old-time melodies on the piano in the corner. And things can ...ever be dearer to an old Scot's heart than on Robbie Burns Night, ...hen the haggis is piped in with all due ceremony, then sliced open ...ith a sword. (New Year's Eve and January's Australia Night are a ...ouple of other special events that many people make bookings for ...*ell* in advance.)

Why bother to fly all the way back to the Sceptred Isle when you ...an have an evening's worth of charm, character and service—and better ...ood—for the price of a meal and a pint of stout at The Crow & Gate?

Beer Trivia

...*e oldest brewery in the world is the Weihenstephen Brewery near* ...*unich, founded in A.D. 1040.*

The Timberland Inn

1680 Timberland Road, Cassidy
Telephone: 245-7541

Hours: 11 a.m. - midnight, Monday - Wednesday; 11 a.m. - 1 a.m., Thursday - Saturday; 11 a.m. - 10:30 p.m., Sunday

The Navigator: Travelling north on the Island Highway towards Nanaimo, turn left onto Timberland Road, directly across from the Air B.C. terminal in Cassidy. The pub is about three blocks up on the right (look for the "Timberland Pub / Beer & Wine Store" sign).

Don't be fooled by the fake-looking "frontier moderne" exterior of **The Timberland Inn**—this relaxed and genuinely funky ale house celebrates Cassidy's pioneer past with a casual verve that many a museum would do well to copy. Huge sawmill blades and a whole wall of swede saws greet you when you enter. Swag lamps and old-fashioned red chairs create a rustic mood, while above the bar is a motley display of homesteading gear—bear traps, wagon wheels, washboards, moccasins, wooden shoes, enamel pots, kerosene lamps and a hefty copper clothes iron—that is part the collection of the owner, part antiques on semi-permanent loan from pub regulars. But don't worry about the hush of the past creating a solemn mood . . . you've just entered one of the friendliest bars on the entire Island!

The bartender usually has some conversation for the guests—even if they're just one-time-only drop-ins from the nearby airport who are pretending that the Timberland is the pre-flight lounge. Even locals who've been coming here for a decade or more may say hi to a newcomer as they mosey over to their customary tables. For this is truly a neighbourhood place, one that seldom gets rowdy—except on weekend evenings, when live music duos crank out dance-happy tunes covering the gamut from country-rock to 1960s pop. And there's some pace to the place during the big twelve-team ball tourney in June

(hoist your glass to that rack of trophies to the right of the bar). More typically, though, it's quieter here; Wednesday night is given over to darts, Sunday afternoons putter along in the cribbage lane, and on Mondays there's free pool all day. Spare some time to eyeball the fun collection of bills above the bar: the currency comes from Mexico and the Netherlands, Trinidad and Hong Kong. Many of the bills are scrawled over with comments, and make for a great read, beer in hand (a $1 bill reads "Here Today, Gone to Tahsis," while an adjoining $2 bill proclaims "We're Back — Tahsis Sucks"; down the way, a habitual heaver penned this cautionary screed: "Dan Got Sick Here Many Times").

With its rough-plank walls and rustic charm, The Timberland Inn offers good food and good cheer to regulars and newcomers alike.

Beer Trivia

During Prohibition, New York City boasted over 30,000 speakeasies.

The Cassidy Inn

Island Highway, Cassidy
Telephone: 245-7095

Hours: 11 a.m. - 1:30 a.m., Monday - Saturday; 11 a.m. - 12:30 a.m., Sunday

The Navigator: Just north of the airport at Cassidy, 7 km south of Nanaimo.

As befits a longstanding local landmark, The Cassidy Inn is comfortably old-fashioned. Its homey, sometimes smoky interior—including those terry cloth covers on the tables—recalls its half-century of service as one of the few roadhouses on the route between Victoria and Nanaimo. "I can remember when I was a little girl, waiting out in the car while my parents slipped in for a quick drink," recalls one of the friendly waitresses. "And now I work here!" These days, although it's still primarily a meeting place for all the thirsty locals, it gets quite a trade in "drop-ins"—in many cases quite literally. For The Cassidy is within screaming distance of the bungy jumping operation that's been set up on an abandoned train trestle a few hundred yards down the highway. And after those thrill-seekers dive a hundred feet towards the river, only to be brought short by a giant elastic band strapped to their ankle, what could be better as a nerve tonic than a few glasses in the nearby ale house? With a crowd ranging from jean-jacketed locals to those swan-diving daredevils with fluorescent "Bungy Zone" T-shirts, this is a pub with a unique ambience.

A somewhat moribund Cassidy was taken over in the early 1980s by the Kellys, who reshaped the old roadhouse into the friendlier, more contemporary format of a neighbourhood pub. The Cassidy changed hands nearly two years ago, and the current owner a young Finlander named Harry Ahokas, has been keeping up the good work. There's a pool tourney on Wednesday nights, but it' the now-legendary Saturday afternoon jam session that continues to be the real signature of this affable ale house. Those 3 p.m. session are a magnet for all the nearby residents, of all ages, who like their country & western with a rocking backbeat; and although the talent level can vary, there's no denying the good times that are inspired by these informal sessions of music making!

Or drop by in quieter times and order something off the menu from the adjoining Cassidy Inn Restaurant. The daily specials are always well received, but the real star of the menu is the chicken fingers, which always sell well. And if you're tired of always ordering pub hamburgers, try the curried shrimp or the lasagna.

Even if you never dial in those radio stations that specialize in tunes by Willie Nelson and Dolly Parton, no highway promenade is complete without paying your respects to this friendly, well-maintained pub.

Beer Trivia

"Steam" beer, the only native American beer style, developed in a nineteenth-century San Francisco devoid of refrigeration. It was brewed with lager yeast at the (higher) ale temperature. This was one of the first beers to be carbonated, and its name derives from the hissing sound that emanated from a newly tapped keg.

Pub Philosopher

"Work is the curse of the drinking classes."

— Oscar Wilde

The Dinghy Dock

Protection Island (Nanaimo)
Telephone: 753-2373

Hours:	Noon - midnight daily, during high season; 4 p.m. - 10 p.m., Monday - Friday, and noon - 10 p.m., weekends during the summer season NOTE: Typically closed November 1 - February 28.
The Navigator:	The Dinghy Dock is only accessible by boat; non-mariners can take the pub's private ferry, which berths a few hundred metres past the Gabriola Island ferry slip, just across from the Harbour Square Mall. The ferry ($3.75) runs hourly whenever the pub is open, leaving Nanaimo Harbour at 10 minutes past the hour.

It's all well and good for West Coast pubs to sport a nautical theme, but no one comes by their marine motifs more honestly than the **Dinghy Dock Pub,** Canada's only floating grog shop. Anchored just off Protection Island, which lies a few hundred metres offshore from Nanaimo Harbour, the Dinghy Dock is the consummate marine pub. The casually funky atmosphere is a treasure trove of brass rails, ship's lanterns, anchors, miniature boats, glass floats, yachting pennants, life preservers and a fancy brass binnacle. In a nice touch, the floor is varnished fir planking "caulked" with white nautical rope. Aside from the cosy indoor seating, you have the option of grabbing your pint and ambling out to the patio section, where zephyrs will tickle you under the chin as seabirds soar and boats bob at anchor. It should be no surprise that this friendly establishment is wildly popular during the five months of summer, when up to 150 pleasure boats find daily anchorage nearby and many of those boaters descend on the Dinghy Dock for lunch, laundry facilities and ice-cold libations.

"We're a summery, sunshine kind of place," says affable owner Bob Banerd, who runs the place with the skilled assistance of his first mate, wife Hilda. "You can hardly *move* in here during July and August," he continues. "We get tourists from all over the world — they steal our

menus and take home our coasters as souvenirs!" A small fortune in bills, which began above the bar and has since spread along the walls to form an informal mosaic alongside the hundreds of beer coasters, testifies to the bar's international appeal.

Although they get their fair share of celebrities—Alan Alda was up last summer, as was some unnamed plutocrat whose 150-foot yacht boasted a carry-along float plane perched aft—the Dinghy Dock is decidedly on the casual side. Aside from the occasional canoeist or kayaker who comes by, Bob recalls one patron who swam over from his boat, equipped with just a bathing suit, a thirst and a $20 bill. "I had to mop up after him," shrugs Bob, "but I didn't mind. We're not about to set any dress code restrictions." With good food and live entertainment on the weekends (including a Scottish piper who sometimes is on hand to herald sundown), this is one pub whose popularity should stay at high tide for a long, long time.

Although most of Bob's customers come from the boating crowd, one of Bob's sons runs an hourly ferry service from Nanimo during pub hours, guaranteeing that mere landlubbers can get in on the action. (Consider making a day of it by taking the connecting ferry to nearby Newcastle Island, a provincial park with great beaches, interesting wild-life and a three-hour perimeter trail.) But whether you arrive in a massive yacht or a skimpy bathing suit, Bob and the Dinghy Dock crew will guarantee you a pleasant time "on board" their unique pub!

Beer Trivia
Canada's first brewery was built in Quebec City in 1668.

The Lighthouse Pub and Bistro

50 Anchor Way, Nanaimo
Telephone: 754-3212

Hours: 11 a.m. - midnight, Sunday - Thursday; 11 a.m. - 1 a.m., Friday - Saturday

The Navigator: Situated in Nanaimo's Seaplane Terminal. Heading north on Nanaimo's Front Street, watch for Anchor Way on the right, just before the Malaspina Hotel.

Nanaimo has always been a little bit, well, patronized by Victoria, and there's no better place to see the error of that arrogance than at **The Lighthouse Pub and Bistro**, which has a million-dollar view overlooking Nanaimo's harbour and Fisherman's Wharf. Sited on pilings over the water, this handsome, six-year-old building boasts the pub on the top level and a fancy bistro on the main floor. They share their prime waterfront real estate with Nanaimo's Seaplane Terminal, and because it is regulated by the Harbour Commission, federal authorities display their usual omniscience by considering the building a vessel. (Pub patrons can rest assured that they're unlikely to be suddenly readied for takeoff, but can admire those nearby seaplanes as they make regular flights to Vancouver and do charter business all over the province.)

Even if you don't get any higher in the sky than the pub, however, that 270-degree view is a dazzler. This picturesque harbour is Nanaimo's true glory (it's better than Victoria's), and Protection and Newcastle Islands add a pretty backdrop to all the fish boats and pleasure craft that ply the waters there. The pub itself intimate and friendly, with an airy West Coast sensibility, offers encouragement to hedonist and philosopher alike. Whether you're kicking back on the sun-drenched outdoor deck or hunkered down a the circular bar, it's hard to find any spot on the Island that provides a more attractive opportunity for creative elbow bending.

And once you've feasted on the view, it's time for more tangible fare. The food here is particularly fine: all the cooking i

done in the bistro kitchen, then beamed up via dumb waiter. Because the Lighthouse Bistro is one of the more elegant restaurants in Nanaimo, you'll be paying a bit more . . . but it's still a bargain. Aside from the regulars like burgers and fish and chips, they have fancy seafood, teriyaki chicken brochette and various pastas. The most decadent item on the menu is lobster thermidor, cooked in a cognac and champagne sauce.

And now, if you're not too full of lobster or too tired from all the sightseeing you've done today, it's time to lace up those hiking shoes. The Lighthouse is poised near the start of the splendid two-mile waterfront walkway that meanders north from Fisherman's Wharf through a sequence of little parks, where it culminates at the public market, hard by two more brew palaces, Muddy Waters and Miller's Landing (see pages 96 and 98). And just 400 metres in the other direction is the launch point for the little ferry that embarks for the Dinghy Dock pub (see page 92) that floats just off Protection Island. Pub crawl, anyone?

Pub Philosopher
"Wine gives great pleasure, and every pleasure is of itself a good."
— *Samuel Johnson*

Muddy Waters Marine Pub

1724 Stewart Avenue, Nanaimo
Telephone: 754-4220

Hours: 11 a.m. - 1 a.m., Monday - Saturday; 11 a.m. - midnight, Sunday

The Navigator: Heading up Stewart Avenue towards the ferry terminal, turn right towards Nanaimo's public market.

"There's nothing dull, grey or boring about Muddy's," boasts longtime bartender Zulu, and the lineups in the evenings are clear proof that a lot of Nanaimo-ites in search of a good time are inclined to agree with her. Perched on barnacle-encrusted pilings right over the water off Stewart Avenue, the charmingly casual **Muddy Waters Marine Pub** overlooks the marina and nearby Newcastle Island. Although a lot of boaters end up slaking their thirst in this funky pub, particularly in summer, you certainly don't need to know your stem from your stern in order to find yourself a happy haven in what is easily one of Nanaimo's friendliest pubs. (In slightly more freewheeling days, Nanaimo took great pride in boasting more grog shops per capita than any other city in Canada.)

With super water views that allow you to savour a colourful armada of fishing and pleasure boats—the outdoor deck is definitely the place to be during summer—some nautical memorabilia are unavoidable . . . but, this being Muddy's, the glass floats and fishing gear are joined with odder items such as a lobster trap and a mournful-looking stuffed heron. A few years ago there were even several fishing holes cut into the floor, but they proved too chilly during the off-season, and were permanently boarded over.

With its heavy-duty post and beam construction and high fir ceiling, Muddy's has a confidently casual air that attracts both dockside denizens and uptown urbanites. Even in the middle of the afternoon, some George Thorogood on the juke and a spirited pool match will enliven your spirits. For this is definitely a party place, and the friendly waitresses take real pride in working here—they even got a fancy Foster's trophy for winning this year's drinks-on-a-tray race, which was part of the Bathtub Week celebrations. (Those other trophies up on the wall reflect the pub's baseball, soccer and hockey sponsorships.)

Owners Ron Hughes and Mickey McGuire—"harum scarum rascals" in the words of one (anonymous) employee—make sure that the Muddy Waters Marine Pub honours the frisky frontier spirit of Nanaimo. With fine food, a great location and good-time crowds, this is one joint that's gonna keep jumpin' for a long time to come.

Beer Trivia

Until the Middle Ages the brewing of beer was done exclusively by women as part of running a household. These women were known as "ale wives." But by the 1400s, men had largely taken over the brewing arts, creating powerful guilds.

Pub Philosopher

A man to whom illness was chronic
When told that he needed a tonic
Said, "Oh doctor dear,
Won't you please make it a beer?"
"No, no," said the doc. "That's Teutonic."

Miller's Landing Pub

1824 Stewart Avenue, Nanaimo
Telephone: 753-4833

Hours: 11 a.m. - midnight, daily

The Navigator: Heading up Stewart Avenue towards the ferry
terminal, turn down to Nanaimo's public market
on the right.

Sited within frisbee-tossing distance of the B.C. Ferries
terminal and the marina, and right at the end of the seawall,
Miller's Landing Pub attracts a mixed, often youngish crowd.
But whether it's joggers or strollers, live-on boaters or delayed
ferry-goers, or maybe a trio of downtown businessmen holding
an informal board meeting over lunch, the varied clientele
certainly agrees that the food and atmosphere make Miller's a
fine destination.

Owner Bill Rudy, who bought the place nearly two years ago,
says, "Our claim to fame is the food—when you come in here, nine
out of ten tables are eating." The menu proudly says that this is a
pub and bistro, and Miller's certainly offers that kind of upbeat,
uptown atmosphere. Hip and modern, with plum and teal accent
colours, varnished wood, a large fireplace open on two sides, and
numerous plants, this contemporary variation on deco design
specializes in casual comfort. And acknowledging the pub's
proximity to the water, there's a fifty-six-pound salmon that looks
a little chagrined to be stuck on the fireplace, as well as
etched-glass sails on the windows that overlook the public market
and the marina (people who want to jig for their own lunch can
seek out the nearby tackle stores, then head for the Nanaimo
public boat ramp).

With reggae and college rock on the stereo and sports TV
above the bar, Bill Rudy ensures that there's a lively spirit to his
pub. He also wants Miller's to be a community-minded place, so
he's continued the longstanding tradition of supporting a local ball
team (aerobic underachievers can make do with the in-house darts

tournament). And the sitdown crowd hasn't been ignored either: Wing Ding Wednesdays offer bargain chicken wings in seven different flavours, while electronic music trivia on Thursdays can quickly find out if you know the difference between Motown and Mick Jagger.

Pub Philosopher

"There was a young girl named Ann Heuser
Who swore that no man could surprise her
But Pabst took a chance
Found a Schlitz in her pants
And now she is sadder Budweiser."

The Windward

1588 Boundary Crescent, Nanaimo
Telephone: 754-7111

Hours: 11 a.m. - 1 a.m., Monday - Wednesday; 11 a.m. - 1:30 a.m., Thursday - Saturday; 11 a.m. - midnight, Sunday

The Navigator: Travelling on the Island Highway through Nanaimo, follow the signs to the hospital. The Windward is located in Beaufort Centre, right next door.

If drinking right next to a hospital makes you feel healthier about what may be happening to your liver, then book an appointment at **The Windward,** which is situated in the Beaufort Centre, immediately beside Nanaimo Regional General Hospital. This cheerfully bustling neighbourhood pub is in a high-density urban area, and it attracts a varied clientele that includes doctors and dietitians, posties and poets.

The atmosphere is West Coast nautical, complete with driftwood dividing walls, lobster traps, glass floats, yellowed maps, crossed oars, brass boating gear and yet another deep-sea diving suit on display (this one has snuck away from the entrance and is now posed rather casually near the men's bathroom). But one of the most attractive features of the Windward focuses not on the sea but the air: there's a ton of natural light that floods in from the skylight-cum-window that runs the length of the pub, and it gives the place an airy grace.

All that natural light gives you a great opportunity to study the menu, one of the better ones on the Island. Aside from the soups and salads, sandwiches, eight different hamburgers, Cajun blackened snapper and chicken stir-fry, there are gourmet snacks like breaded mushrooms and ethnic nibbles from Greece and Mexico. Sunday and Tuesday you can stand in line with all the regulars, who are hungrily waiting for the roast beef and Yorkshire pudding special. And if you decide to pass on church some day, bow your head

before a scrumptious plate of seafood Benedict, which is the real catch of their Sunday brunch.

And their beer "menu" has been prepared with equal care. Aside from a great selection of bottled beers from around the globe, their draught taps pipe in a fine selection of the best B.C. brews.

The Windward has been treating its customers well for close to a decade now, and its traditions of fine food and good service embody the true spirit of a neighbourhood pub.

Pub Philosopher

An alcoholic is a man you don't like who drinks as much as you do."
— *Dylan Thomas*

Jingle Pot Pub

2211 Jingle Pot Road, Nanaimo
Telephone: 753-4223

Hours: 11:30 - midnight, Sunday - Thursday; 11:30 - 1 a.m., Friday - Saturday

The Navigator: Heading north on the Island Highway through Nanaimo, turn left onto Bowen Road, then left again onto Wakesiah Avenue (at the traffic light); turn right onto Jingle Pot Road and keep going for 1.9 km.

You know that you're onto something when people who are snugly ensconced in one fine pub suddenly start raving about the food in another pub ten miles away. Ditto when other pub *owners* take the time to praise a rival establishment. The final evidence of an exceptional kitchen comes when a pub builds up a regular takeout business. Such is the case with **The Jingle Pot Pub**, which has been fattening up enthusiastic Nanaimo residents (and many others besides) for five years now.

Despite the "wild west" walkway out front—courtesy of the building's original owner, whose tack shop has long-since been out of business—The Jingle Pot proves to be pretty modern inside, albeit with a few funky touches such as brass carriage lanterns and some old-timey photos. Rock-faced columns, blond wood and tastefully muted wallpaper set the mood in this attractively high-energy establishment, which typically boasts a lineup during dinner hours.

Owners Rick and Eileen Wood make sure that the "food and service are great," and the crowds have responded by making this one of the most popular dining destinations in all of Nanaimo. Probably the biggest seller on the menu is the fish and chips, which can be ordered in three sizes (but you'd have to be a third-generation logger to tuck away that awesome three-pieces-of-fish platter). "No one has ever, ever left here hungry," boasts Rick, who served up more than 50,000 pounds of halibut last year. An ex-firemen and still a commercial fisherman, Rick used to catch all his own fish till two years ago—business is just too busy these days. Chimes in Eileen, "We've started serving coffee to the people waiting in those weekend lineups, just so they won't go away."

So, what else comes out of this ridiculously popular kitchen? People trying to kick the french fry habit could order the halibut burger and salad instead of those fish and chips. There are five types of Caesar salad, a great seafood platter, juicy steaks, a dozen sandwiches and many daily specials. Anyone whose stomach isn't operating at full capacity could opt for finger foods such as zucchini, clam strips or the Mexican potato skins.

"This is a friendly place," says Rick, who deliberately avoids the distractions of live music so that the customers can come here to talk and socialize. "This is a people place—you're made to feel at home whether you're wearing blue jeans or a suit and tie."

As long as you can leave your diet at the door, no pub tour of Nanaimo is complete before you've dropped into The Jingle Pot Pub and paid your respects to one of the finest kitchens on the Island.

Beer Trivia

The term "bootlegger" stems from the high boots that drinking men wore during Prohibition. The fancy boot-tops concealed secret compartments where booze could be stashed.

Pub Philosopher

"Once, during Prohibition, I was forced to live for days on nothing but food and water."

— W.C. Fields

Piper's Inn

4520 Hammond Bay Road, Nanaimo
Telephone: 758-4462

Hours: 11 a.m. - midnight, Monday - Thursday; 11 a.m. - 1 a.m., Friday - Saturday

The Navigator: From Nanaimo, take Departure Bay Road, off the Island Highway. Turn onto Hammond Bay Road and go 4.2 km to Piper's. From the north, turn onto Hammond Bay Road at Woodgrove Shopping Centre intersection and follow along for 4.8 km.

If you want to visit a real neighbourhood pub while in Nanaimo, then point your roadster in the direction of **Piper's Inn**. But you don't have to be a local—or a Scot—to become part of the clan at this fine and friendly establishment. Whether you're looking for a plate of home-cooked food, a glass of ale or maybe just the pleasures of an old-fashioned British-style pub, they're always available at Piper's.

The wood floors, dark wooden tables and chairs, post and beam construction, stained glass and a sequence of brass carriage lanterns create the ambience of an Old World public house. A set of bagpipes mounted on the wall acts as an emblem for Piper's, while a series of photos of British pubs adds to the atmosphere (one classic grog shop is poignantly called "The Last Drop"). Plants are dotted throughout the spacious interior, and a handsome fireplace can heat up even the dreariest and dampest of our West Coast winter days.

Owner Ruth Dancy has been nurturing her bar since 1979, and she's built up a loyal local clientele that includes business types, retirees and some of the scientists who build up a thirst working at the nearby Biological Research Station. An ever-growing collection of $1 and $2 bills continues to creep along the big beams that spread out from the massive bar—it's an informal insurance plan for patrons who may inconveniently find themselves tapped out some night at last call.

104

The food is worth checking out here, particularly the prime rib on Friday nights, but it's the regulars who benefit the most: it's easy for them to be available for the numerous special events such as Robbie Burns Night, New Year's and Halloween ("Scare up some friends," reads the poster over the bar). Piper's sponsors a mixed fastball team, but more people get involved with the less aerobically demanding dart squad, which plays weekly in a five-pub league. Although the live music was let slip for awhile, they're moving back towards having musicians on the weekend, ranging between country-flavoured M.O.R and some classic "graffiti" pop/rock.

With its close proximity to the Departure Bay terminal, this pub has lots to offer ferry passengers who would otherwise be making do with industrial-grade coffee and sandwiches. But whether you're headed for Vancouver or just taking in the gorgeous, off-Highway scenery on the lower Island, don't forget to heed the sweet call of Piper's Inn.

Beer Trivia

The expression "to hob-nob" likely comes from the time of Henry VIII, when there was a fashion for beer that had been warmed on the hob of the fireplace grate. Thus the thoughtful host would take his beer orders as: From the hob or not?

Tommy Gaskin raised a keg of beer weighing 138 pounds above his head 656 times in a six-hour period, on October 28, 1989.

The Black Bear

6201 Dumont Road, Nanaimo
Telephone: 390-4800

Hours: 11 a.m. - 12:30 p.m., Sunday - Thursday; 11 a.m.
                          - 1:30 p.m., Friday - Saturday

The Navigator: Take the Island Highway 8 km north of Nanaimo
                          city centre (just beyond Long Lake), turn left
                          onto Rutherford Road and immediately right onto
                          Metral Drive. Go 1.5 km, turn left onto Dumont
                          Road; pub is .5 km on the left.

Those seeking the pleasures of a pub in pastoral surroundings need look no further than **The Black Bear**, which sits on a grassy slope above Brannen Lake. The rear deck offers relaxing water views, while the surrounding trees give a sweet sense of carefree seclusion, far from the worries of the city. With its friendly mix of regulars and, increasingly, the tourists who have heard good reports along the grapevine, this newly christened pub offers the chance to mix convivial social pleasures with a keen appreciation of the beauties of nature.

Although regular Island Pubbers will remember this place as the Harp and Shamrock, it was bought in October of 1989 by John and Linda Wicks, who used to run the Dinghy Dock, the floating pub moored at Protection Island (see page 92). Originally from England, the Wicks have brought over some of the classic British pub traditions with them. They've made The Black Bear more like a neighbourhood pub and less like a bar, with darts night on Mondays and Wednesdays (and it has already paid off in the form of trophies from the five-pub dart league they're part of). The new owners also made sure that the kitchen would become a goodwill ambassador by offering big portions and significantly better meals than had been the case. And as a further reminder of England, two import draughts grace the taps: Tetley's Bitter and Double Diamond.

There are oak and pine tables and chairs, a dark-beamed ceiling and a massive, two-sided brick fireplace that is decorated with steins, an intriguing collection of horse brasses and an unapologetically rude snapshot of two bears doing what comes naturally during the heady days of spring. It's a cosy place, complete with such bric-a-brac familiars as plates over the mahogany bar and a row of colourful ceramic heads dotted along a beam, staring quizzically towards the fireplace.

Add in the chance to retreat to eleven acres of soul-restoring nature, an excellent selection of draught beers, a mouth-watering menu (everything from calamari and jalapeno-spiced french fries to fish and chips, seafood melt and the hefty Black Bear "Brrr Grrr"), and you've figured out why so many people have put The Black Bear on their pubbing short list.

Island Trivia

Nanaimo's courthouse was designed by the celebrated Francis Rattenbury, who earlier came to fame through his work on both Victoria's Parliament Buildings and the Empress Hotel. Rattenbury was later murdered in England by his chauffeur, who was having an affair with his wife.

Pub Philosopher

"Romance, like alcohol, should be enjoyed but should not be allowed to become necessary."

— Edgar Friedenberg

The White Hart

Foot of North Road, Gabriola Island
Telephone: 247-8588

Hours: 11:00 a.m. - 12:30 a.m., Monday - Thursday; 11:00 a.m. - 1:30 a.m., Friday - Saturday; 11:00 a.m. - 11:00 p.m., Sunday

The Navigator: Just a 20-minute ferry ride from Nanaimo, the White Hart is located 50 metres up from the ferry dock (round-trip for walk-ons is $2.25).

One of the easiest ways to get a taste of the good life on Gabriola Island is to leave your car behind and hitch a ferry ride over from Nanaimo and pay a visit to **The White Hart Pub**, which is located a scant fifty metres from the ferry dock. (But if you enjoy touring by auto then a tour of this pastoral island retreat is definitely recommended.)

Its dockside location at the point of entry for Gabriola means that the White Hart is the unofficial meeting ground for full-time locals, summer residents and visitors alike. Upon entering this funky and friendly establishment, first-timers will be drawn to the dozen and dozens of beer steins hanging from the roof beams, as well as the old-fashioned beer trays hung high along the walls and colourfully trumpeting the virtues of such noble British brews as Bass and Mackeson. But all the pubbing paraphernalia takes a back seat to the 170-year-old stained glass window from an original White Hart pub in England (this beauty is mounted a little out of sight, just behind the bar).

Like many pubs, the White Hart takes pride in presenting a menu that emphasizes quality at a fair price. This used to be a restaurant called The Beanery till it evolved into a pub in 1984, and those traditions of quality food and service have continued to earn the place fans from all over the island. The bracing Caesar salad is super (for garlic lovers only!), and the charbroiled hamburgers have that genuine homemade heft. Those seeking a lighter bite could opt for the nachos or the Greek salad, while the pan-fried oysters are a good reminder of just how pleasant life on the West Coast can be.

The outdoor deck is a popular spot during summer: shaded by umbrellas, visitors can sip their frosty drinks and keep an eye out for eagles and seabirds in between noting hourly visits by the ferry. Inside there is a separate games room, where darts, pool and video diversions are available. During the off-season, an airtight stove makes sure that the chill stops at the door. This is the best time to see the locals about their business: the crib tourney is into its seventh year—up to twenty-four players confront the pegboard on Wednesdays—while the ever-active darting contingent comes in the following night. And because the last ferry leaves for Nanaimo at 10:15 p.m., visitors can long savour their White Hart pleasures, postponing saying goodbye to scenic Gabriola till well after twilight.

New Year's Day of 1990 was a sad day for White Hart owners Annette and Marv Sweeney—that's when these seventeen-year veterans sold their beloved pub to Ron McCaffrey and Terry Towns. But even though they now come here as customers and not owners, it's satisfying to them that the new owners haven't changed a formula that has so successfully served locals and visitors alike for nearly twenty years.

Beer Trivia

The largest beer tankard ever was made by the Selangor Pewter Company of Kuala Lumpur. It stands six-and-a-half feet high and has 615-gallon capacity.

The Thrasher

Port Silva Marina, Gabriola Island
Telephone: 247-8044

Hours:	11:00 a.m. - 1:00 a.m., Monday - Saturday; 11:00 a.m. - midnight, Sunday
The Navigator:	Head straight up from the ferry dock at Gabriola, continuing along South Road to Silva Bay Road (15 km); turn right and it's a short hop to the Marina.

Gabriola is one of the friendliest of the Gulf Islands, and this is nowhere more apparent than at **Thrasher's Pub**, located in the scenic Port Silva Marina. Although it began life as a restaurant, Thrasher's became a marine pub in the early 1970s. This isn't one of your designer pubs—it's more like a casual rumpus room than anything—but the whole point of it are the good times available in the pub and the pretty sailing views to be had out those dockside picture windows. One of the locals shows off his Rude Boys Club T-shirt. "We're protectors of the environment," he explains with smile. "Give us enough to drink and we'll protect anything!" But beneath the friendly frivolity, what he and the other locals have been protecting is one heck of a boating destination. This sixty-berth marina gets packed during the summer: sailors come from all over the Northwest, and there's always a strong Mainland presence because the Royal Vancouver Yacht Club owns Tugboat Island, just a few hundred yards offshore. Rare is the day when the knotty-pine walls of Thrasher's don't echo with the sounds of marine good cheer.

Port Silva is a dream to sail into—if you can get moorage. There are a swimming pool, sauna and hot tub available to relax in, fine food in the Clubhouse Restaurant, plus a laundromat and boutique. Even if you haven't cracked your boat up lately, take a peek at the repairs going on in the fully operational shipyard. And don't overlook the equally active "shipyard" contained right in the pub itself. Retired boatbuilder Harvey Giles is busy in his little shop every day, crafting miniature "Newfoundland" dories out of cedar

(These beauties come up to four feet in length and make fine gifts.) At the other end of the sailing spectrum, the ninety-two-foot *Spirit of Chemainus* is a permanent resident. This brigantine-rigged training vessel, an official Tall Ship modeled after a 1902 sloop, is available for charters and tours—just the thing for landlubbers who arrive by car and want to get a taste of adventure on the high seas.

During the off-season, it's mostly locals here, but the fun continues. They often have movies on Monday nights, while Tuesdays the dart teams let fly. Thursday is typically jam night, with host Little Davey presiding over whichever musicians are brave enough to plug in and let the good times roll. And the food is fine all the time.

So whether you're eager to join the throngs during the sunny days of summer or are doing some off-season island hopping and just want a drink amongst some truly friendly company, set your course for Thrasher's Pub.

Beer Trivia

Nova Scotia, as recently as 1983, police could raid a home and seize all the liquor present if the occupants were spotted drinking beer their own backyard.

Pub Philosopher

A man who is building a house is really building a tavern for his friends. "

— *Norman Douglas*

Lantzville Village Pub

1527 Lantzville Road, Lantzville
Telephone: 390-401?

Hours: 11 a.m. - 1 a.m., Monday - Saturday; 11 a.m. midnight, Sunday

The Navigator: Several kilometres north of Nanaimo on the Island Highway, turn right onto the Lantzville cutoff, just past the Woodgrove Centre; the pub is 1.4 km along, in the heart of Lantzville.

The Lantzville Village Pub is one of the real treasures along the Island's pubbing circuit. Built in 1924, the pub was extensively renovated in 1989 after it was purchased by Ted and Fay Anderson (who also own The Prairie Inn, see page 38). There are very elaborate coved ceilings with recessed lighting, a dozen hanging philodendrons, fancy ceiling fans, nautical and sports prints on the walls, fancy French doors that open onto a glassed-in patio, modern colour scheme in beige and taupe, and brass rails. A handsome bar made of dark wood (imported years ago from a saloon in Missoula, Montana) helps recall the frontier past when Lantzville was a mining town and, later, a logging centre. Although it's come a long way from its early days as the Lantzville Hotel, the tastefully refurbished pub still functions as the heart of this friendly community of just over 3,000 souls—aside from providing the town's most attractive social forum, they also sponsor a men's fastball team, host a fishing derby and support a men's and women's golf tourney. The Lantzvillians are justifiably proud of a community where there's no need to lock the doors at night . . . so don't try to tell them that they're now just a suburb of Nanaimo!

The single most striking characteristic of The Lantzville is the magnificent water view, with the sun glinting off the Strait of Georgia. The Winchelsea Islands occupy the foreground, while the snow-dusted peaks of the Coast Mountains hold up the sky over the horizon (on a clear day you're seeing as far as Sechelt). It should be no surprise that this pub's regulars hail from as far away as Parksville and Ladysmith—if you want food, drink and good times in comfortable surroundings, it's hard work to come up with a better destination than The Lantzville. Aside from the daily specials, the menu favours those same wonderful, diet-destroying hamburgers (such as the infamous "belly buster") that have been feeding the locals for years at the Prairie Inn in Central Saanich.

In these post-Expo days, it's getting harder to remember when British Columbians weren't allowed to drink on Sundays. Decades ago, that was never a problem in Lantzville. It was generally understood that on the sabbath, the pub simply migrated to the kitchen, with the knowing patrons sneaking in by the back door. Even on-duty members of the Provincial Police weren't above slaking their thirst at this illegal—but undeniably popular—watering hole.

Today, of course, all that gets broken at The Lantzville Village Pub is the occasional diet and vow to have "just one glass"—be warned, it's all too easy to fall under the spell of this beguiling pub!

Beer Trivia

England quickly established itself as an island with a definite thirst. By the mid-1800s there were more than 130,000 licensed brewers in England, with London alone boasting more than 300 breweries.

Pub Philosopher

"Alcohol is like love: the first kiss is magic, the second is intimate, the third is routine. After that you just take the girl's clothes off."
— Raymond Chandler

Parksville and Area

~

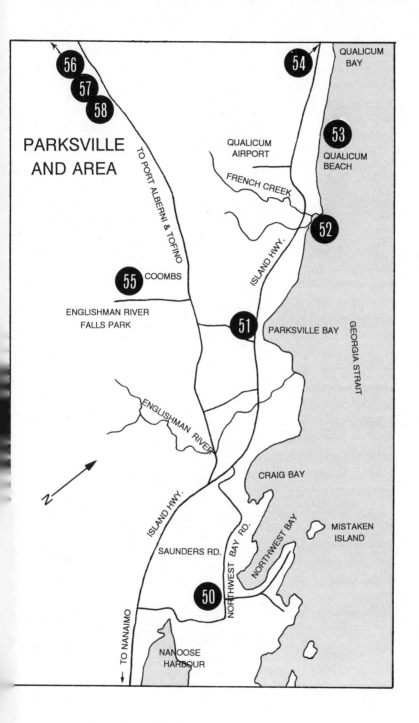

PARKSVILLE
AND AREA

QUALICUM
BAY

QUALICUM
AIRPORT

QUALICUM
BEACH

FRENCH CREEK

TO PORT ALBERNI & TOFINO

ISLAND HWY.

COOMBS

ENGLISHMAN RIVER
FALLS PARK

PARKSVILLE BAY

GEORGIA STRAIT

ENGLISHMAN RIVER

N

CRAIG BAY

MISTAKEN
ISLAND

NORTHWEST BAY

ISLAND HWY.

SAUNDERS RD.

NORTHWEST BAY RD.

TO NANAIMO

NANOOSE
HARBOUR

The Rocking Horse Ranch

Sanders Road, Nanoose
Telephone: 468-7631

Hours: 11 a.m. - 12:30 a.m., Sunday - Thursday; 11 a.m.
                    - 1:30 a.m., Friday - Saturday

The Navigator: Heading north from Nanaimo on the Island
                    Highway, go 11 km past Woodgrove Centre
                    and turn right at the Nanoose traffic lights
                    (look for a Petro-Canada station). Continue
                    along Northwest Bay Road for 4.5 km, then
                    turn left onto Sanders Road.

Although Vancouver Island doesn't lack for unusual pubs, one
of the real stand-outs is **The Rocking Horse Ranch**, a uniquely
"western" pub located on a functioning ranch that specializes in trail
rides and horse boarding.

The pub itself is a casual pastiche of cowboy funk, with
plank floors, a stuffed pheasant and a handsome set of bull horns
mounted over the fireplace. The windows look out over thirty-one
acres of pasture and a huge horse barn, complete with an indoor
riding ring; and near to that is a newly renovated rodeo arena
(Visitors to the Island may be intrigued by the grove of
red-barked arbutus trees, which are unique among deciduous
species in that the bark molts while the leaves are retained
year-round.) Between the trail animals and the boarders there are
usually twenty or more horses on the premises, and they're often
indulging in spirited play in the fields. Several dogs and a
unusually friendly goat round out the livestock.

The Rocking Horse Ranch is the scene of some great annual
events, including one of the Island's best rodeos. Near the end of
August, up to 2,500 fans crowd the arena to watch chaps-clad
cowboys put some beautiful horses through their paces. And not all
the action is earth-bound: the Annual Skydive Boogie, which
attracts aerialists from all over Western Canada, Washington and
Oregon, is the traditional kick-off for this memorable weekend

ess competitive equestrians can head out on the daily trail rides, and arties of ten or more can make reservations for a fun-filled hayride.

If all this sounds intimidatingly like a dude ranch ... don't worry! Those who care more for pubbing than palominos can stay ndoors for many a happy hour—aside from a fine menu, there are arts, video and pinball games, occasional crib tournaments and live usic on the weekends. Also on the weekends is their justly famous utdoor summer barbecue, which features a steak dinner for the low rice of $5.95 (no wonder they sell more than a hundred dinners on good night!).

Whether your Pinto runs on gas or hay, whether you drop in a parachute or drive up in a BMW (or get let off at the E & N ilway stop 300 metres away), you're always welcome to share in e good times at this unique Island pub.

***

Beer Trivia

one monastery cum brewery, the Latin inscription on the wall nslates to: "There is no beer in heaven, so we drink it here."

117

The Sand Bar

Island Highway, Parksville
Telephone: 248-4744

Hours: 11:30 - 12 midnight, daily

The Navigator: Located in the Island Hall Hotel, right on the Island Highway in the heart of Parksville.

For decades the Island Hall has been a leader in the hospitality industry on Vancouver Island, esteemed for both its food and the quality of the seaside accommodation. Not one to fall behind Parksville's most famous hotel notched up its service considerably in July of 1990 by opening **The Sand Bar**, a posh pub that is very much in the English tradition. Edwardian in style (like a toned-down Christie's Carriage House), the one large room features understated elegance highlighted with deft touches of sumptuous luxury. Hardwood floors, wool carpeting, spiffy mahogany millwork, brick fireplace with a copper hood and a textured ceiling create mood of bygone luxury. Elaborate tear-drop hanging lamps and fabric-covered wingback chairs complete the feeling that you've dropped in for a glass of port with your rich old uncle, and he's just ushered you into the study of his 1920s-era mansion.

There's an outdoor deck that affords charmed views of beach expanses that are lapped by the sparkling blue of the Strait of Georgia, while the Coastal Mountains stand tall at the horizon edge. Seated out on the balcony, glass in hand, it's easy to see why Parksville continues to be such a successful tourist magnet. But energetic manager Manfred Renz isn't about to let those views do all the work. His kitchen is famed for its very generous portions with a menu that includes fish and chips, burgers, seafood and gourmet snacks like potato skins and the shrimp plate. The week-day lunch specials attract bankers, realtors and other business types. But if you'd rather apply your knife and fork to some more serious dining, consider dropping in on Thursday night for the "pasta lover's dream," an exotic Italian buffet for $7.95 that's available from 6:00 to 9:30 p.m.

Some of the other traditions that this brand-new pub has instituted include trivia night on Mondays, darts on Tuesday evenings and local live entertainment on Wednesdays. Expect more professional tunes on Friday night, while Sunday afternoons feature a toe-tapping jazz session from 3:00-6:00 p.m. Add in the friendly staff, one of the Island's most classic views and a gourmet selection of beers on tap (including Hermann's, Bass Ale from Britain and Germany's Dab), and you have more than enough reasons to visit The Sand Bar, one of our newest and most attractive pubs.

Island Trivia

)uring the early days of Victoria's Union Club (before it moved to its
~resent posh location), there were frequent Saturday night rat chases, as
~e higher-spirited members turned rodent control into a drunken sport.

Pub Philosopher

Drinking makes such fools of people, and people are such fools to
~egin with, that it's compounding a felony. "

— *Robert Benchley*

The Boar's Head

French Creek House, Lee Road, French Creek
Telephone: 248-3713

Hours: 11 a.m. - 11 p.m., Monday - Saturday; noon - 6 p.m., Sunday

The Navigator: Located at French Creek Marina, halfway between Parksville and Qualicum (turn right at the giant red arrow advertising the Morningstar Golf Course).

The Boar's Head Pub is located halfway between the thriving resorts of Parksville and Qualicum, where it's tucked into French Creek House, a lively camping/fishing complex that offers complete accommodations for both vacationers and fishing folk. It's no coincidence that there are nearby chartering facilities, boat ramp, and a government wharf: there's great fishing to be had in the Gulf, particularly during the summertime when the tough-fighting Coho salmon move through the area en route to the spawning rivers. But you don't have to have spent the day scrapping with trophy salmon in order to enjoy sinking into a comfy lounge chair at The Boar's Head, glass in hand.

Cosy as a rec room, with wood floors, maps on the brick walls and tabletops made from whole "rounds" carved from a big tree, The Boar's Head declares its fondness for the outdoor life with stuffed pheasant and a few multi-point deer heads. But pride of place, right over the massive stone fireplace, goes to "Boris," the pub's ferocious-looking namesake and mascot. This 1,200-pound boar hailed from nearby Lasqueti Island (no, he wasn't running wild!), and many of the pub regulars are quite affectionate to the toothy old fellow. Both Lasqueti and Texada Islands form part of the panoramic beach and seaviews to be admired from the comfort of The Boar's Head.

The kitchen takes pride in serving up food made "from scratch," and the menu goes beyond the standard to include such fare as shrimp quiche, lasagna and deep-fried mushrooms. Because

of suites located just above the pub, the regular live music has been put on hold. But there's still a piano sitting in the corner, and some of the locals, including one boat-dwelling fellow who lives on the dock, will sit at the eighty-eights and play a medley of good-time tunes, anything from Gershwin to Elton John.

The fishing gets a thumbs-up all year round from most anglers, and fresh seafood is sold right at the docks. French Creek Resort also has an ambitious sports complex, complete with swimming pool, sauna, jacuzzi, gym and weight room. If you pack away the pasta, maybe consider burning off a few of those calories before heading back to the highway . . . . And don't overlook Hy'emass House Gallery, just fifty metres away. It has a great collection of contemporary and traditional Indian arts and crafts, including woven baskets, silkscreens, silver jewellery and totems.

As you're booming up the Island Highway towards French Creek, consider angling for a plate of homecooked food and a pint of frosty refreshment under Boris's watchful eye. The Boar's Head awaits!

Beer Trivia

Shortly after the Spanish Conquest, the first brewery in the New World was established in New Mexico by Spanish forces.

The Shady Rest Hotel

Island Highway, Qualicum Beach
Telephone: 752-9997

Hours: 10 a.m. - 11 p.m., Monday - Thursday; 10 a.m. -
                    midnight, Friday - Saturday; 10 a.m. - 9 p.m.,
                    Sunday

The Navigator: Located right on the highway, at the north end of
                    Qualicum Beach.

No drive past Qualicum is truly complete without a stop at **The Shady Rest Hotel,** which is plunked down right on the beach and boasts some of the finest views on the Island. Although the pub has been recently renovated—including an attractive outside wall mural, a lyrical seascape incorporating whales, salmon and seabirds such as herons and gulls—there's some intriguing history to mull over as you sip a beer. Until the summer of 1985, this establishment had been owned and operated by the Kincaide family, who built it in 1924. The Kincaides are generally credited with being the first whites to homestead the area, with the original Thomas Kincaide and wife Sally arriving by ship in 1882. Two years later, Thomas Junior was born, not quite ready to help his pioneering parents with the land-clearing and house-building chores.

The second Thomas eventually did make his mark, however, by inaugurating The Shady Rest Hotel on July 8, 1924. The business fell to his son, Gerald Thomas Kincaide, during the Second World War. A fourth-generation Thomas Kincaide carried on the family tradition until the mid-1980s, at which point the historic building was sold to outside interests.

The current owner is Wayne Duncan, who came to his new post after learning the trade at The Prairie Inn, an extremely popular brewpub in Saanichton (see page 38). His attractively understated renovations—including oak millwork, a stone chimney that backdrops an airtight stove, and old-time photos—have made the pub more comfortable without adding any jarringly modern notes. And the sundeck he added emphasizes the pub's superb marine vistas, which look out over Georgia Strait towards Lasqueti and Texada Islands.

One thing that hasn't changed is the fine food, which comes from the same kitchen that services the adjoining restaurant. From seafood fettucini and shrimp omelettes to steak sandwiches and daily specials, meals at The Shady Rest have a home-cooked quality. The atmosphere, too, remains friendly and relaxed. Whether you're a summertime visitor, there to quaff a pint and watch the leisurely action on the beach, or have dropped in during the off-season and end up cheering on the Tuesday night pool and dart teams, you'll find that The Shady Rest is a genuine haven by the sea.

Beer Trivia

During Prohibition, companies sold vast quantities of malt extract, ostensibly for the manufacture of bread but largely to fill the demands of home brewers. One manufacturer included this tongue-in-cheek "warning" on his label: "Do not allow yeast to come in contact with this product. To do so will cause it to ferment into beer."

The largest single brewing organization in the world is Anheuser-Busch of St. Louis. It has 12 breweries in the United States, and in 1989 it sold 9.5 million litres.

The Crown & Anchor Pub

Island Highway, Qualicum Bay
Telephone: 757-9444

Hours: 11:30 a.m. - midnight, Monday - Saturday; 11:30
                    a.m. - 9:00 p.m., Sunday

The Navigator: This one's easy—it is right on the Island
                    Highway, just 2 km north of the Big Qualicum
                    River bridge.

Even though it started off in 1904 as a girls' school, and passed through later incarnations as a roadhouse and restaurant, **The Crown & Anchor** has long since found its true identity as a "working man's" bar— one whose friendly comforts have found favour beyond the Qualicum Bay/Bowser locals to include both wintertime skiers and summertime hordes of beach-seeking tourists.

Substantial renovations in the 1970s and early 1980s have created a pleasing ambience that recalls the spirit of an English country pub, complete with brick walls and dark beams. There is wall-to-wall carpeting, rustic leather and wood chairs, lots of plants and a massive maple bar decorated with stained glass and highlighted with carved wooden panels appropriated from Hy's Mansion in Vancouver. Two large fireplaces add some wintertime warmth, and a well-lit glass trophy case bears tribute to a longstanding tradition of sports sponsorship. In all, The Crown strikes an immediately cosy feeling, as though you've just stepped into someone's living room or den.

Current owner Rick Martin, who used to run Bimini's pub in trendy Kitsilano, has a casual style that fits in with the neighbourhood. He supports local hockey, football, baseball and curling teams, while his satellite dish brings in a lot of TV sports—and also brings in most of the area's armchair athletes, who congregate to cheer on their favourite teams. Tuesday night is dart league, there's a pool tourney on Wednesday evenings, and all the cribbage experts settle in for a long session on Saturday afternoon. When I ask him what special events the pub has on its calendar, an eavesdropping regular seated nearby barks out: "We had a wet T-shirt contest once . . . till Rick ran out of spit!" The affable owner puts a wry smile on his face, as if he's unsure whether to lob back a matching insult or else buy the rascal a beer to compliment him on his rude wit.

Aside from sprucing up the place with a bit of a facelift when he took over in March of 1990, Rick also renovated the kitchen. The fish and chips and seafood chowder are top sellers, and the (now) fresh-made burger patties have regained their popularity. Add in the daily specials and tasty finger foods such as nachos and Cajun shrimp, and you've got lots of good reasons to seek a temporary berth at the always friendly Crown & Anchor.

Beer Trivia

Cuneiform tablets record brewing in Mesopotamia as early as 6000 B.C. About forty percent of their barley crop was devoted to beer making, and wages were partly paid in liquid form.

Pub Philosopher

"So who's in a hurry?"
    — Robert Benchley, in response to a warning that drinking is a "slow poison"

The Frontiersman

Alberni Highway, Coombs
Telephone: 248-9832

Hours: 11 a.m. - 1 a.m., Monday - Saturday; noon - midnight, Sunday

The Navigator: Located smack in the heart of Coombs, about 6 km west of Parksville along the Alberni Highway.

Just a few hours drive up from Victoria, **The Frontiersman Neighbourhood Pub** is the heartbeat of Coombs, a funky rural community that comprises loggers, fishermen, small-scale farmers and other such folk who take real pride in working for a living. And when they want to play they descend on this charmingly rustic pub, a sprawling log cabin of a place, lit with electrified kerosene-style lamps and decorated with swede saws and other such logging gear. Above the bar the sign reads: "If your wife calls and you're not here—*you* tell her!"

In the time it takes to drink just one beer you'll catch on to the friendly and happy rhythms of this charming town. The Frontiersman has been successfully slaking thirsts for a quarter-century now, but they've had less luck with the baseball team they sponsor: there are but a few trophies over the fireplace. As the bartender notes with an amused shrug, "We don't do all that well." Luckily, it's one of the few areas where Coombs comes up short.

The food is great at The Frontiersman, and the atmosphere has loads of appeal, but there are plenty of other good reasons to visit Coombs, particularly in summer. A couple of rodeos are held in the area, as well as other equestrian events, and cowboys and cowgirls head to the pub to sluice that trail dust out of their throats. Bluegrass music almost seems like an industry up in these here parts: their annual Bluegrass Festival attracts top-draw pickers and singers from all across B.C. and the western United States, and the crowds throng in to hear those dobros and fiddles playing traditional mountain music. (A lot of this music-making has rubbed off on the locals, who have dances every Thursday through Sunday in The Frontiersman.)

Even if there's nothing special on during your visit, wander down and check out the nearby Farmer's Market—it's the sod-roofed building with the goats on it! And consider buying a loaf of bread at one of the most respected bakeries on the entire Island.

Whether it's summertime in the outdoor beer garden or winter has gripped the Island and you are gratefully toasting your toes in front of a crackling fire, The Frontiersman will always make your visit worthwhile.

Beer Trivia

In the United States in the 1930s, a few regional breweries began to distribute their product nationally. Shipping their brews to far-off markets cost a "premium" that was added to the local price. Slick advertising soon ensured that "premium" beer became synonymous with "better," and the public was happily paying more for beer that was often inferior to the local brew.

The Fish and Duck Pub

8551 Bothwell Road, Sproat Lake
Telephone: 724-4331

Hours: Noon - midnight, Monday - Thursday; noon - 1 a.m., Friday - Saturday

The Navigator: Follow the highway through Port Alberni and look for the pub's prominent sign. Turn left off the highway onto Faber Road, and keep following the periodic signs to the pub.

Lovers of pastoral beauty won't want to overlook this cosy lakeside retreat, which is set amidst the fir trees at the edge of Sproat Lake. **The Fish and Duck Pub**, which also operates a marina, is a mecca for both the 2,000 lakeside locals and all the boaters, campers, fishing fanatics and other outdoor folk who flock here during the summer, attracted by the peaceful atmosphere and excellent recreational opportunities.

There are a couple of mascot mallards that waddle happily about the dock and yard, proudly showing off their latest brood of ducklings. During summer, you may want to follow their example and stay outdoors too. If so, then travel no farther than the sundeck, where a frosty beverage will make those lake and mountain views even more attractive. Notes the bartender: "A lot of tourists come in for one beer, and end up contentedly sitting on the deck all day!" If you're lucky, you'll get to see a bit of an air show courtesy of the Martin Mars Bombers, the legendary firefighting water bombers that are based just across the lake.

This decade-old pub was renovated in 1990, and it's more comfy than ever. There are leather chairs and wooden tables, two suspended wagon wheels garlanded with electric lamps, and a fireplace and airtight stove to keep the customers warm after winter socks in. They also give new meaning to the term "big-screen TV" by projecting the hurtin' songs of the Nashville Network onto a wall screen originally designed to show slides.

The Fish and Duck has new owners, ex-Victorians Aaron and

Sheila Griffin. Even though Aaron used to be a tree faller and Sheila worked in a nursing home, this young couple has already caught on to the hospitality business in a big way. Service here is genuinely friendly, and the kitchen serves up all the pub standards plus more unusual items such as Mexican food, pasta specials and the veggie dip on the finger food menu. The summer barbecues should be sizzling again next year, while the off-season is given over to regular pool tourneys.

Whether you arrive via Chrysler or Chrisscraft, seek the summer pleasures of the outdoor deck or the homey comforts indoors, there is always a warm welcome, a cold pint and tranquil beauty awaiting you at The Fish and Duck Pub.

Beer Trivia

Sake, Japan's national drink, is typically thought of as a wine. However, because of the way it is brewed, it must be classified as a beer.

Pub Philosopher

"One of the disadvantages of wine is that it makes a man mistake words for thought."

— *Samuel Johnson*

The Westwind Pub

4940 Cherry Creek Road, Port Alberni
Telephone: 724-1324

Hours: 11 a.m. - 1 a.m., Monday - Saturday; 11 a.m. - midnight, Sunday

The Navigator: Coming into Port Alberni, take the right fork of the highway, following the signs to Tofino. About a mile down, look for the Alberni Mall on the left, then turn left at the Safeway and the Payless station.

If you think there's nothing new to be done about decking a pub out in a nautical theme, then you'd better set sail for Port Alberni's **Westwind Pub**, which has elevated what could have been mere kitsch decoration into real folk art. The foyer contains a deep-sea diver skulking behind a bent and rusty ship's ladder—and he's just a hint that you're about to take a real plunge into maritime lore and history. The pub proper is festooned with all the regular stuff such as Japanese glass floats, pulleys, a brass ship's telegraph and signal light, fishing lures and a ship's lantern. There are also antique maps and paintings, irregularly framed in hemp rope, that seem to have drifted in from *Treasure Island*. The divider walls are built of driftwood, and some of the inside walls are planked with salvaged wood—look for the telltale toredo worm holes. Above the sixteen-foot handcrafted oak bar are some huge old *National Geographic* maps of the world.

Opened in July of 1987, this friendly establishment is very much cast in the mould of a neighbourhood pub. There is an amazing menu (pasta to potato skins, escargot to calamari) and quick service, which has paid off in an ever-increasing lunchtime trade and a cadre of faithful regulars who appreciate the good times to be had in this bright and airy pub. Wednesday night is chicken wing night, while Sunday sees a return to tradition with the always popular prime rib dinner.

Manager Susanne Rogers makes sure that all the patrons—be they regulars or passers-through who have dropped in en route to

Long Beach—are well looked after. With darts and cribbage, the sunny outdoor patio (or the gigantic stone fireplace during winter), the about-to-be-added beer and wine store, and that amazing menu, there are any number of reasons why thirsty landlubbers should chart a direct course to the Westwind!

Beer Trivia

In medieval times when a woman got married, her family brewed a special celebratory ale that was used to toast the happy couple. This "bridal ale" is the source of the modern word "bridal."

The Blue Heron Inn

Weigh West Marina, 643 Campbell Street, Tofino
Telephone: 725-3277

Hours: 11 a.m. - midnight, Monday - Saturday; 11 a.m. - 11 p.m., Sundays; (expect reduced hours in winter)

The Navigator: Located on the waterfront as you drive into Tofino.

The rugged beauty of the west coast of Vancouver Island is one of our greatest treasures, and nowhere is this more apparent than at Long Beach, the most famous tourist attraction on the entire Island. Now incorporated into Pacific Rim National Park, Long Beach has long been a magnet for campers, hikers, fishermen, kayakers and outdoors lovers of all kinds. Whether they've come to watch the migrating grey whales, go scuba diving or salmon fishing, or capture on camera the dazzling panorama of this West Coast wildness, no visitor leaves untouched by the fierce grandeur of the area's abundant natural gifts.

Set amidst all this splendour, **The Blue Heron Inn** at the Weigh West Marine Resort in Tofino provides a perfectly civilized counterpoint and a chance to catch your breath—and have a meal and a beer—as you cherish your day of exploration and discovery.

Erected on pilings at the edge of Tofino Harbour, this relatively new pub has been sensitively designed to complement its natural environment. With hefty post and beam construction, teal walls and a blue bar, wicker and wood chairs, and contemporary Indian art on the walls, the Blue Heron seems to embody the spirit of Tofino. But the pub doesn't bother trying to draw too much attention to itself: its wall of windows and the outside seating area direct your eyes to the magnificent marine views and surpassing natural beauties for which this area is justly famed. The nearby island is Meares, which became a celebrated battleground between loggers and an Indian-environmentalist coalition in the mid-1980s (the preservationist forces won out in the end).

The food here is some of the best you'll find, with great daily specials

and all the regular fare, such as fish and chips, steak sandwich, chili and hamburgers. Not surprisingly, there's a seafood emphasis to the menu, including shrimp and chips and a half-crab served hot. And crustacean connoisseurs who get crabby unless they do their own cooking can purchase their mouth-watering dinner-to-be live from water pens down at the wharf.

While you're poring over maps and guidebooks as you sip your beer in the Blue Heron, do consider taking one of the whale cruises: in spring you can observe the grey whale migration, while summer finds them feeding in both the inland waters of Clayoquot Sound and the open Pacific off Long Beach. There are also boat rentals and fishing charters. And don't be so overwhelmed by the natural beauty that you forget to check out the longhouse-shaped art gallery of famed Indian artist Roy Vickers, located just down the street. This superb artist has brought West Coast Indian art to new levels of international respect, and his unique gallery is regarded by many as a shrine.

Truly, no trip to our West Coast can be considered complete until you've paid your respects to Pacific Rim National Park and the Tofino-Ucluelet area. The stunning beaches, abundant wildlife and towering first-growth forests make this charmed environment a truly unforgettable place to visit. And after a day rich with adventure and discovery, seek out the classy comforts of the Blue Heron Inn, where fine food and pleasant company will take on a little bit of the magic the area has been so generously blessed with.

Beer Trivia
Beer cans were first introduced, by an American brewery, in 1935.

Courtenay and Area

~

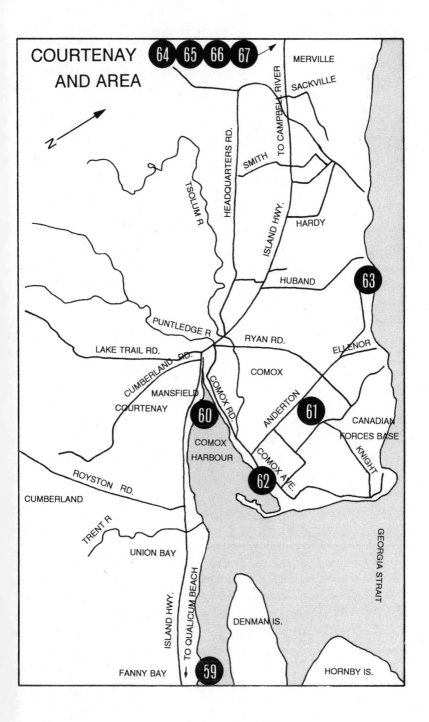

COURTENAY AND AREA

64 65 66 67

N

MERVILLE
SACKVILLE

TO CAMPBELL RIVER

HEADQUARTERS RD.

SMITH

ISLAND HWY.

HARDY

TSOLUM R

HUBAND

63

PUNTLEDGE R

RYAN RD.

LAKE TRAIL RD.

ELLENOR

CUMBERLAND RD.

COMOX

MANSFIELD

COMOX RD.

ANDERTON

COURTENAY

60

61

CANADIAN
FORCES BASE

COMOX
HARBOUR

KNIGHT

ROYSTON RD.

COMOX AVE.

62

CUMBERLAND

TRENT R

UNION BAY

ISLAND HWY.

TO QUALICUM BEACH

GEORGIA STRAIT

DENMAN IS.

FANNY BAY

59

HORNBY IS.

135

The Fanny Bay Inn

Island Highway, Fanny Bay
Telephone: 335-2323

Hours: 11 a.m. - 11 p.m., Monday - Saturday; 12 noon - 8 p.m., Sunday

The Navigator: There's no missing this distinctive landmark at the southern end of Fanny Bay (on the water side, just 20 minutes north of Qualicum Bay).

Recently painted a bright blue, the ever-reliable **Fanny Bay Inn** has been a landmark roadhouse since it was built in 1938. Even though the original clientele of loggers and sawmill workers has been replaced by summer tourists, skiers, business folk and, of course, the current crop of locals, this friendly pub has always lived up to its reputation as a charming country inn that's worth a leisurely visit.

Inside, the F.B.I. resembles an old farmhouse, one where you've just dropped in to have a neighbourly chat. There's a battered old piano and a fireplace in one corner, with mugs hanging off the beams and a collection of colourful old trays set on the moulding near the ceiling. Cosy and unpretentious, the F.B.I. has a clientele that ebbs and flows with the seasons. The regulars hail from Deep Bay to Comox, and during the slower months, the bartender knows nearly everybody in the joint. But things get hopping during the summer, while at the height of ski season and during the herring runs (the dock's within staggering distance) there's standing room only.

The food here is good, generous and reasonable. The clubhouse is their classic sandwich, while lighter biters can go for the salads. The weekend dinner specials are always popular, and include the New York steak and prawns or else the good and greasy "rack-o-ribs." Those who want to "dine local" should try either the clam chowder or the oyster dinner (six pan-fried beauties, plus coleslaw, toast and fries). And we're not sure whether this qualifies as food or drink, but the brave of heart—and stomach—may want to

take a ride with an "oyster slider," which is basically a Caesar with a raw oyster lurking at the bottom of the glass.

The present owners are Dave and Betty Hopkins, and in their three-year tenure they've added on an outdoor beer garden, complete with horseshoes, barbecue pit and steak specials. Dave's brother is a magician, and Dave himself has a few tricks up his sleeve—he's not above picking on some hapless inebriate at a corner table and making scarves disappear or some such. And when he's really on a roll, he'll take a mirror off the wall, have both himself and his current victim face each other with the mirror on edge between them, and then somehow create the illusion that they're flying (and depending on how much alcohol's been consumed, the illusion can get pretty hilarious!).

But there's no magic in the Fanny Bay Inn's continuing popularity: by being genuinely friendly and offering tasty country hospitality, this classic roadhouse can look forward to another fifty successful years.

Pub Philosopher
"Drink because you are happy, never because you are miserable."
— *G.K. Chesterton*

The Whistle Stop

2355 Mansfield Drive, Courtenay
Telephone: 334-4500

Hours: 11 a.m. - 1 a.m., daily

The Navigator: Coming into Courtenay from the south, watch for Mansfield Drive on the right (you'll have two chances, as both ends of this half-circle road connect with the Island Highway).

The Whistle Stop Pub, plunked down near Courtenay's Comox River estuary, will offer a pleasant half-hour to any Island Pubbers passing through the Comox Valley. Although its train days are far behind (there used to be a nearby railway stop), a small rail engine replica over the entry and the "Whistle Stop" name itself still recall the days when a rail link was vital to this bustling mid-Island town.

Upon boarding this friendly pub, you'll note a near-maze of pine booths that are surmounted with brass rails. Large windows and skylights let in the light, while the solidness of the huge beam construction is offset by groupings of hanging plants. A fireplace and brick hearth and copper hood add a cosy touch in one corner, while games-minded folk can visit either the pool or the darts nooks (both of which are decorated with long rows of Grand Marnier bottles). A large-format digital display board adds a contemporary touch—and occasional laughs—when its big red letters list the current crop of NSF cheque offenders, who are asked to clear their accounts at the bar.

In some ways, the Whistle Stop feels like a "guys" place particularly during the live-music weekends or when the joint gets buzzing with the energy of the après-ski crowd, still high from those thigh-burning runs down the steeper faces at Mount Washington. But today's high-energy pleasures haven't entirely displaced a sense of the pub's railway past. There are two train murals, one in the pool nook and another near the bar. Attractive stained glass shows off the Whistle Stop locomotive logo, while a giant station bell suspended just above the bar seems to be waiting for some cheerful inebriate to send it pealing. And distributed throughout the place are archival black and white photos that illustrate how important the railroad was during the early settlement days in the Valley.

Summer time is worth a visit just to sit in the outdoor patio, making the day's vacation plans over a frosty beer. And if you're coming back from a hike up Forbidden Plateau, or maybe have had a tough day of arm-wrestling coho out on the saltchuck, then grab a menu and tuck into some of the fine food available here (light biters can go for the nachos or veggie dip, while bigger appetites may wish to tackle the baron of beef or the veal parmesan).

Summer or winter, the Whistle Stop provides comfort and pleasure to locals and wayfarers alike.

Beer Trivia
In earlier days, some serious sippers used to drink out of "whistle tankards"; when they were running low on the suds, a sharp blast on the whistle (attached to the brim or handle) ensured a prompt refill.

Pub Philosopher
"I exercise great control and never touch any beverage stronger than gin before breakfast."

— W.C. Fields

The Leeward

649 Anderton Road, Comox
Telephone: 339-5400

Hours: 11 a.m. - 1 a.m., Monday - Thursday; 11 a.m. - 1:30 a.m., Friday - Saturday; 11 a.m. - 12:30 a.m., Sunday

The Navigator: From Courtenay follow the signs to Comox, then watch for Anderton Road on the left, two blocks past the hospital. (Overhead signs point to Powell River ferry and CFB Comox.) Pub is on the left, 1.2 km up Anderton Road.

Wave-tossed Vancouver Island has a unique coastal charm, and that rugged beauty is the theme of **The Leeward Pub** and Brewery. Built in 1976, on the site of the first school built on the Comox Peninsula, this popular neighbourhood pub set sail with its present nautical theme in 1980, under the captaincy of owners Gil and Ron Gaudry. The bleached wood exterior and those driftwood fences marking the patio perimeter offer first-time visitors just a taste of what's in store inside.

Upon boarding the Leeward, an ocean notion is everywhere apparent. A deep-sea diver stands guard at the entrance (it's a wonder, given all the drysuit-equipped pubs on the Island, that any *real* diving gets done anymore), while the inside is stem to stern nautical memorabilia. Aside from the two-candle binnacle, a genuine porthole, a large ship's telegraph (made from 300 pounds of brass), a manual foghorn and the regular gear like Japanese floats, there's also a wall-length painting of the Battle of Trafalgar. Giant maps and driftwood that's been roped together to form half-walls complete this truly charming salute to the West Coast.

The Leeward constructed its own brewery in 1984, thereby becoming the fourth brewpub in all of Canada. Currently there are four custom beers on tap: a bitter, a lager, a pilsner and the Dark British Ale (the lager is the most satisfying, at least to my taste). Self-taught brewmaster Bob Lamb uses malt extract instead of mashing his own grain, and produces about 400 kegs a year. The brew is pumped directly to the bar taps through 350 feet of beer lines, and is also available as off-sales in one-litre bottles (the Leeward was the first brewpub in Canada to get an off-sale licence). Bob is proud of his malt mastery, and instructive brewery tours are available on Saturdays.

But probably the best reason to book a cruise with the Leeward is the excellent food. There's a big menu—everything from cod Florentine, clams and scallops to eight different burgers and other such "landlubber delights" as beef stroganoff, ribs and Mexican food—and both the quality and quantity get top marks. Add in all the cosy nooks and crannies, the big stone fireplace and the separate pool room, and there's no denying that the Leeward should be on every Island Pubber's shortlist.

Island Trivia

When Victoria's Crystal Garden opened in 1925, there were no bars or taverns allowed in the city. Not to stifle the party spirit entirely, management arranged that underneath each table was a slot perfectly designed to accommodate a mickey of liquor. Although these slots were ostensibly to store the women's purses, they were typically used for their real, anti-Temperance purpose.

The Black Fin

132 Port Augusto (top of Comox Wharf), Comox
Telephone: 339-5030

Hours: 11 a.m. - 12:30 a.m., daily

The Navigator: Take the Island Highway through Courtenay, then follow the signs to Comox. Continue along Comox Avenue, then turn right onto Port Augusto.

Comox has more than its fair share of quality pubs and restaurants, and none seems to have generated more waves than **The Black Fin**, a marine pub sited at the top of Comox Wharf. Only two years old, this classy establishment presents a winning combination: great views and even better food. At present there's an Edwardian, masculine feel to the pub—it has simple, elegant lines and more than $60,000 in gorgeous mahogany millwork—but a decorator will be coming in soon to soften things up a bit by adding drapes and such. With its massive mahogany bar, a large brick fireplace complete with a distinctly non-nautical musk-ox head (souvenir of the old Elks Hotel, which burned down on this site a few decades ago), and a wall of windows that looks out over the postcard views of Comox Glacier, Baynes Sound, Mount Arrowsmith and Hornby and Denman Islands, the Black Fin is definitely in the limousine class of pubs.

"We're pretty well the busiest restaurant in town now," states the happy manager, who gives most of the credit to master chef Jerry Patterson, who has twice been featured in the *Vancouver Sun* and who perfected his craft working at the Hotel Vancouver and Victoria's esteemed Empress Hotel. The menu presents itself as "a catalogue of culinary delectables for perusal and sustenance," and the food actually lives up to all that purple prose. Caesar salads are great here, as are the snails. The wide-ranging bill of fare starts with standards such as burgers and fish and chips, but quickly reveals this master chef's interest in more exotic pleasures, including garlic ginger prawns and blackened redfish (in all, there are four "ragin' Cajun" dishes)

And aside from the regular menu, there are about a dozen specials that get changed every few weeks.

Boaters with a taste for trophy-class cuisine can dock at the attached Black Fin Marina, which has twenty-eight berths, a gas dock, public showers and a laundromat. Of course, this marine pub has earned a lot of loyalty amongst the landlubber set, too. The pub sponsors various teams, including darts, curling and hockey, while its tennis league boasts 110 racquet-toting members. The clientele here is an easy-going mix, from fishermen to landlocked yuppies whose only interest in the sea is how good the sole Florentine is that night.

And despite the luxuriousness of the place, the Black Fin has added just a hint of rigour for those who are interested: to take advantage of those superb views, the outdoor deck runs year-round—except during *really* nasty weather—and management hands out pads and blankets to all comers who want a frostily intimate communion with the great outdoors.

Editor's Note:

Fire destroyed the original Black Fin Pub this winter, however we understand that the pub will be rebuilt as quickly as possible.

Beer Trivia

Some of the older names for beer include "barley broth," "oil of barley," and "barley water."

Pub Philosopher

"Claret is the liquor for boys; port for men; but he who aspires to be a hero must drink brandy."

— *Samuel Johnson*

The Griffin Pub

Little River Road, Comox
Telephone: 339-4466

Hours: 11 a.m. - 12:30 a.m., Monday - Thursday; 11 a.m. - 1:30 a.m., Friday - Saturday; 12 noon - 8 p.m., Sunday

The Navigator: Follow the signs directly to the gate of Comox Airforce Base, then turn left along Little River Road; pub is approximately one mile along, on the right.

Because it sits smack up against the air strip for the Canadian Forces Base in Comox, **The Griffin Pub** is in its fullest glory during the annual Comox air show or when the Snowbirds are practising their daredevil aerobatics. But there are many other reasons to visit this fine drinking establishment than just the hope of seeing our F-18 fighters zipping through the skies.

Even though those shrieking jets make it apt that this pub be named after the fierce mythological bird of prey, the Griffin's mascot is a suit of armour, which makes a rather droll guard just outside the pub. Discovered by the owner's aunt at a garage sale and promptly nicknamed "Sir Percy," this steel-plumed custodian has a few informal touches, including sneakers and a hockey stick standing in for the battle ax that some shameless sot pinched after a drunken revel.

If Sir Percy lets you in, you'll discover one of the Island's friendliest neighbourhood pubs. While owners Roger and Donna Guy have happily acknowledged that their biggest source of customers sits right next door—there's a fascinating selection of airplane photos on the wall, plus some other military memorabilia—their pub has numerous civilian fans from all over the Courtenay-Comox area. Just five years old, the Tudor-style building has literally a thousand or more exotic beer coasters, elegantly patterned along the beams, wall and ceiling. There's a three-high row of currency that spans the bar, and a few of the novelties include a $2 bill folded into a bow tie and somebody's final U.I.C. cheque, valued at a hefty $1.

The pool table is free, and there's a donation jar used to buy a new rag when the green felt gets worn. Like all real neighbourhood pubs, there are lots of traditions here, including the popular summer barbecues (steak, garlic bread, and potato and tossed salad for $4.95). During winter they have a charity chili cook-off, where teams fork over $20 to enter, then brew up their best batch. After a winner is declared, the chili goes into one massive pot and is then sold by the bowl—last year, more than $2,000 went to the Children's Christmas Fund. And whenever anyone gets posted away from the base, all his or her military mates descend on the Griffin for a spirited "mug out."

The velvety Guinness stout—the only available in a hundred-mile radius—is a strong drawing card, but a lot of people will also drop in for the fine food. Whether you opt for the Reuben sandwich or finger food like the deep-fried mushrooms, the kitchen won't disappoint. And leave room for dessert—the pub's signature treat is the "Little River Rock," a baseball-sized scoop of ice cream that takes the plunge in the deep frier for twenty seconds. It, and the Griffin Pub itself, are unique charmers.

Beer Trivia

n seventeenth-century France, the doctors must have been in league with the brewmasters; some of the ailments for which they prescribed beer included grippe, typhoid and even smallpox.

Salmon Point Marine Pub

Salmon Point Resort, Oyster Bay
Telephone: 923-7272

Hours: 11 a.m. - 11 p.m., Monday - Thursday; 11 a.m. - midnight, Friday - Saturday; 11 a.m. - 10 p.m., Sunday (reduced hours in winter)

The Navigator: Located halfway between Courtenay and Campbell River, 1 km north of the UBC experimental research farm. Turn right off the Island Highway, just north of Oyster River.

Vancouver Island doesn't lack for spectacular sea views—or pubs that are sited to take full advantage of our unique marine geography—and some of the best armchair viewing can be had from the blissful comfort of the **Salmon Point Marine Pub**. That 180-degree vista of the Strait of Georgia is damn impressive, all right, especially out on the patio, but stick around for more than one pint and you'll probably see some of the resident eagles dive bombing each other . . . or maybe just settling an old score with an insolent seagull. Pods of killer whales are not uncommon in these waters, and an even more spectacular marine activity happens occasionally. (During August of 1990 the nearby river was too low for the migrating salmon, and the shallows right outside the pub were swarming with fish—and up to fifty "fishermen" at a time, some wearing just bikinis, all desperately trying to scoop up a free dinner.)

The pub itself is West Coast modern: massive beams and a soaring fir ceiling on the slant create an airy, naturally lit spaciousness that recalls a lodge. There's upholstered alcove seating along the walls, plus a scattering of wooden tables, while a profusion of plants adds splashes of vivid colour. The unique bar top is a single, massive slab of red cedar. The obligatory jumble of fishing floats, flags, maps and contemporary Indian art may make for a less-than-convincing coastal pastiche, but Salmon Point's genuine and easygoing charm is seduction first-class. A handsome, two-sided fireplace, built of smooth beach stone, offers near-narcotic comfort during the nasty days of winter.

Nature lovers have dropped into the right place. There are forty-five minutes of well-signed trails through the woods to Woodhus Slough, while birders may be fascinated by nearby Mitlenatch Island, a renowned bird sanctuary. There are two eighteen-hole golf courses within a few minutes' drive, and Salmon Point Resort itself boasts a 200-boat marina, RV park, cottages and fishing charters.

Built up an appetite with all that outdoor activity? Consider tucking into the seafood fettucini, a savoury shrimp croissant, sole neptune or maybe some more terrestrial cuisine such as the veal schnitzel or the ribs. Lighter bites range from chicken fingers to nachos and prawns.

There's occasional live music, but you're more likely to hear some impromptu keyboard riffs as a patron wanders up to coax a few songs out of the piano in the corner. But there will be nothing finer than sitting in peace, hand clasping a mug, as a velvet dusk settles over the Georgia Strait that you've been admiring for the last few hours. It's no wonder that most visitors vow to return to Salmon Point!

Beer Trivia

Czech hops are esteemed by brewers around the world; more than one hundred countries import them to ensure top-quality beer.

Pub Philosopher

"Always carry a corkscrew and the wine shall provide itself."

— *Basil Bunting*

The Royal Coachman

84 Dogwood Street, Campbell River
Telephone: 286-0231

Hours: 11 a.m. - midnight, Sunday - Thursday; 11 a.m. - 1 a.m., Friday - Saturday

The Navigator: Driving through Campbell River, watch for the Hospital signs. Take Second Avenue off the Island Highway, continuing along to the first traffic light past the hospital, where you turn left onto Dogwood. Royal Coachman is just a block down, on the right.

Even though Campbell River is justly famed as one of the great fishing destinations on the West Coast, many Islanders who live as far away as Victoria associate this bustling town—and maybe a few extra pounds around their tummy—with its other claim to fame: **The Royal Coachman** and its celebrated kitchen.

Started in 1978 by Ken and Sylvia Phillips, the Royal Coachman combines elegant, old-fashioned architectural design and workmanship with the most evocative of British pub motifs, including oriental carpets, horse brasses, stained glass, old maps, square antique carriage lanterns, china plates and a noble deer head. "Olde English" hunting prints and scenes of stately carriages complete the mood of a confident British Empire taking an easeful day off. Although the place is too darned big to qualify as "cosy," the seating mostly runs along the walls and successfully creates a feeling of semi-privacy. In the hot months, take a stroll to the outdoor patio—you'll get to it by walking over a bridge that spans a giant goldfish pond. During winter you may feel drawn to the warmth in the semi-circular pit, which is pleasingly arrayed around a dancing fire in the big brick fireplace.

Out-of-town fans of the Coachman who haven't visited it for a few years may feel they've already had a few drinks as they pull up in the parking lot. When the pub was expanded in 1988, it was painstakingly disassembled and rebuilt on the other side of the road.

with office space and a beer and wine store added for good measure. (Old-fashioned mortise and tenon construction permitted such liberties.) The Coachman is considered the first Island pub to have emphasized great cuisine, and despite the relocation, those all-important culinary standards remain intact. The self-serve kitchen offers a core selection of menu standards, but has built a reputation for the rotating daily specials. (They feature several dishes, changing daily, from a repertoire of literally several hundred.) Whether it's seafood quiche, escargot, clam chowder or teriyaki chicken, the food here consistently reaches very high standards indeed.

A real cross-section of people consider the Coachman a favoured old friend. States the manager proudly, "The regular lunchtime crowd ranges from grandmothers to fishermen, and everybody in between." So whether you've been building up a ferocious appetite scrapping with trophy salmon out on the chuck all day, or are just seeking a wee dram to rinse the travel dust off your tongue, rest assured that The Royal Coachman will tend to your needs with courtly finesse.

Beer Trivia

The Women's Christian Temperance Union, which grew to have world-wide influence, was founded in Cleveland, Ohio in 1874.

The Willows Pub

521 Rockland Road, Campbell River
Telephone: 923-8311

Hours: 11:30 a.m. - midnight, Sunday - Thursday; 11:30 a.m. - 1:00 a.m., Friday - Saturday

The Navigator: Heading north into Campbell River on the Island Highway, look for Rockland Road on the left. Follow the road up for several blocks. Pub is on the left, discreetly tucked into a low, brick building.

Although there are numerous *technical* requirements for a neighbourhood pub, surely the single most important element is how much it contributes to the pleasures of fellowship in the surrounding community. By that standard alone, **The Willows Pub** would be a welcome addition to any neighbourhood on the Island. Located in a quiet residential corner of Campbell River, this cheery modern establishment immediately creates a mood of relaxed conviviality. From brass kettles on the hearth and hanging plants, to a summer sundeck and rustic oak chairs, The Willows recommends itself for a leisurely sipping session instead of just a quick drink. Best of all, owners Al and Sue Thulin make you feel like a welcome guest in their home, even during the brisk lunchtime hour.

"I know personally sixty to seventy percent of the patrons here," says Al. "It's mostly people from the neighbourhood, as we're a bit out of the way for the tourists." The Willows has a reputation as a social centre, and the regular, slightly older clientele regards the place as an ideal spot to trade local gossip over a frosty pint. To that end, there's nothing noisier than the dart board to distract patrons. "We don't have banging and crashing and beeping from any video games," declares Al. "This is a place for people to talk—it's not an amusement park!"

The *other* secret to a successful pub is the food, and The Willows has earned an enviable reputation for its hearty meals. There is a good choice of finger foods, and the cheeseburger is legendary, but many regulars look for the dinner specials, which typically cost $7-$8, but go up to $15 for filet mignon. In all, there are about 150 rotating meals that "chef de cuisine" John Zuk conjures up in the busy kitchen. One of his classics is the fish pot, a savoury fish stew that includes prawns, salmon and red snapper; this dish is so popular that there's a "request" list of customers to phone whenever the fish pot's rotation comes round. And red meat traditionalists look forward to Saturdays, which are always prime rib night.

And even though you're unlikely to use the public notice pin-up board just inside the entrance to the pub, it's just one of the telltale indicators that establish The Willows Pub as an outstandingly friendly establishment, one where customers are truly valued and the conversation is as fine as the food.

Island Trivia

Until Prohibition in 1917, public intoxication was most common in Victoria. Drinks were two for a quarter, saloons were everywhere, and there was even a lager beer wagon — kind of a predecessor to the Good Humour truck — that toured the streets, ever-ready to "refresh the inner man."

Pub Philosopher

"I only drink to make other people seem interesting."

— George Jean Nathan

The Landing

Quathiaski Cove, Quadra Island
Telephone: 285-3713

Hours: 11 a.m. - 1:00 a.m., daily (reduced hours in winter)

The Navigator: Pub is on Quadra Island, just 200 metres up from the ferry dock at Quathiaski Cove. Walk on the ferry at Campbell River. If coming from the Cortes Island side of Quadra, just follow the signs to the Campbell River ferry. Moorage is available by the ferry dock if you're coming by boat.

Nothing sums up the spirit of the West Coast better than life on the Gulf Islands, and you'll get an immediate whiff of driftwood and the promise of unpredictable pleasure when you stroll into **The Landing**, which serves as the "neighbourhood" pub for the 3,500 residents of Quadra Island. It's also popular with the residents of Campbell River and the Comox Valley, who regularly take the fifteen-minute ferry ride in order to relax in this funky, get-away-from-it-all place.

Built fourteen years ago as a soup and sandwich joint, it was transformed into a pub six years after that. With its log cabin construction, knotty pine and cedar walls, and rustic furniture, The Landing deliberately harkens back to a pioneering past (the pub is built around the chimney of one of Quadra Island's first homesteads). There's a fireplace at one end of the pub—ideal when a blustering November wind drives you to seek shelter—while the middle of the place is dominated by a handsome, semi-circular bar that was hand-built by a local artisan. Knick-knacks like old bottles and ceramic jugs, tucked into odd corners of the pub, add some casually apt atmosphere. A large "games" room was added on in the mid-1980s, featuring pool and darts (there are four boards, to accommodate the various men's and women's leagues that enthusiastically compete here).

The clientele is certainly eclectic, especially during summer when millionaires, up for the world-class fishing, stand in line with the local crabbers to order lunch and a brew. During tourist season The Landing is tied to the rhythms of the ferry, as every hour yet another load of hungry and thirsty passengers descends. Because they serve close to 400 customers on the busiest days, the chef has introduced a buffet lunch to accommodate the crowds. The food here is truly popular—so many fishing guides and boat charters drop in for provisions that the pub now has its own moorage spot reserved down at the dock. During the off-season, though, the place belongs to the locals; and if you drop in for the pizza special on Friday and Saturday nights, you can join in as they dance to live music or try their exhibitionistic skills at karaoke.

There's lots to do on Quadra Island, including visits to nearby Rebella Spit Provincial Park and the museum of Kwakiutl culture (which celebrates the Island's original inhabitants). And after all that exploring and poking around, leave lots of time to imbibe some unique island culture at The Landing before heading homeward via the ferry.

Beer Trivia

Three saints are patrons of beer: St. Augustine, St. Nicholas (a.k.a. Santa Claus) and St. Luke (in this case, the doctor does know best).

Pub Philosopher

"There is nothing wrong with sobriety in moderation."

— *John Ciardi*

Gulf Islands

~

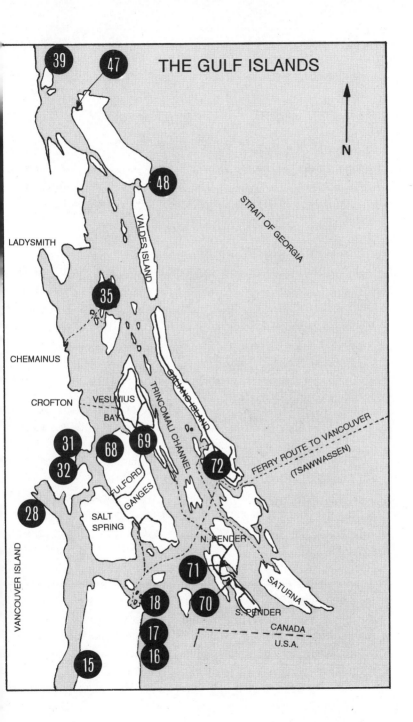

THE GULF ISLANDS

N

STRAIT OF GEORGIA

LADYSMITH

CHEMAINUS

CROFTON

VESUVIUS
BAY

VALDES ISLAND

GALIANO ISLAND

TRINCOMALI CHANNEL

FERRY ROUTE TO VANCOUVER
(TSAWWASSEN)

FULFORD

GANGES

SALT
SPRING

N. PENDER

SATURNA

S. PENDER

CANADA
U.S.A.

VANCOUVER ISLAND

Inn At Vesuvius

Vesuvius Bay, Saltspring Island
Telephone: 537-2312

Hours:	11:30 a.m. - 12:30 a.m., Monday - Saturday; 11:30 a.m. - midnight, Sunday
The Navigator:	Follow the signs to Vesuvius Bay, on the northwest side of the island. Or walk on the Crofton/Vesuvius ferry, which docks right next to the pub.

For more than a half-century, yachtsmen have used the distinctive red roof at Vesuvius as a reference point when heading south towards Sansum Narrows. So when the original inn burned down in 1974, the neighbourhood pub that was built to take its place was consciously styled after the original landmark. (The fine work was by the late Peter Cotton, a Victoria restoration architect responsible for such buildings as the Saint Andrew's Cathedral at the corner of Yates and View.)

The trademark red metal roof of **The Inn at Vesuvius** makes it easy to spot from the sea—but you don't have to be a struggling mariner to take pleasure when you hove into view of this friendly pub. With stunning panoramic views of Stuart Channel that stretch from Sansum Narrows to Ladysmith Harbour, this is one establishment that can charm any visitor without even trying hard.

Inside, The Inn is a bright, cheerful place offering patrons a choice of several distinct environments. First, there's the games area with darts and such. The main section of the pub features that magnificent view (but during the summer you'll probably hope to be one of the lucky ones parked out on the deck, enjoying that scenery in the fresh air). More scholarly students of good ale may choose to cloister themselves in the library: the cosy sofa and chairs invite you to read something from a whole shelf of travel books, and the dark wood walls and some interesting stained glass work of sailboats on a storm-tossed sea create a relaxing atmosphere.

John Teagle's extensive beer bottle collection got marched out the door last year, only to be replaced by more indigenous vessels: check out the mantle above the fireplace, which displays the fine ceramics of local potter Mark Meredith. And there's an interesting story about the bill collection behind the bar. On opening night in April, 1979, an expatriate Kiwi came in and slapped a New Zealand dollar on the bar, saying that if he could buy a beer with it, he'd buy fifty more. That Kiwi dollar is still there, amid currency from all around the globe.

Whether you arrive by boat or bicycle, seaplane or mobile home, the laid-back atmosphere and amiable service at this pub will soon convince you that you're drinking among friends. And after sampling those fine, home-cooked meals, there may be more than a few regrets as the red roof of the Inn at Vesuvius fades from view.

Beer Trivia

During the late seventeenth-century, Harvard University's first president was eventually dismissed because he proved unable to consistently fulfill a key part of his contract: supplying the students with a weekly ration of beer and bread.

A quality home brew will cost its maker approximately $ .33 per twelve-ounce bottle.

Moby's Marine Pub

120 Upper Ganges, Saltspring Island
Telephone: 537-5559

Hours: Sunday - Thursday, 10 a.m. - midnight; Friday - Saturday, 11 a.m. - 1 a.m.

The Navigator: Heading north out of Ganges, turn right on Upper Ganges Road, just past the edge of town.

Acting on the principle that it's never too late for our largest Gulf Island to have its own marine pub, **Moby's** opened for business in the summer of 1990. With cathedral-high ceilings and windows that let in a ton of light, this is an elegant addition to the expanding list of pub choices on the Islands. Perched above the Saltspring Marina at Harbour's End, Moby's has chosen not to clutter the walls with a lot of seafaring kitsch; instead, it lets those handsome harbour views and all the boats bobbing at anchor provide the necessary nautical atmosphere.

As Saltspring's first and only marine pub, Moby's offers showering, laundry and provisioning facilities to the various boaters who put in at Ganges. There's also one hotel room in case any yachters want to temporarily leave the sea behind for the pleasures of dry land. But you certainly don't need to come gliding up in a fancy forty-footer to be made welcome at this fine establishment. The first time we were there, the full house included a trio of bicyclists plotting their route on a map, while nearby two locals were laughing over a crib game and a few glasses of dark beer.

Moby's Marine Pub has been a hit since the day it opened, and one of its best drawing cards is the food. With items such as Louisiana lamb curry and cioppino (a robust Italian seafood stew) on the menu, it's obvious that this is not your typical grog shop! The burger platters are truly awesome (there's even a fresh salmon burger), while less hearty eaters can nibble at a range of appetizers. And don't overlook their occasional barbecue events on the waterside deck, which add some sizzle to the summer sunshine.

Even though Saltspring has been feeling its share of urban-style growing pains, the not-to-be-missed Saturday market in Ganges is still a bustling microcosm of go-your-own-way West Coast charm. After the hawkers have persuaded you to buy some handmade jewellery or maybe a tie-dyed shirt, set your sights on the nearby Moby's Marine Pub, where a tall glass of ale will help you contemplate the pleasures of island living.

Island Trivia

The first recorded settlers in the Gulf Islands were a group of American blacks who had bought their freedom in the U.S. and petitioned Governor James Douglas in 1857 for permission to homestead on picturesque Saltspring Island.

Pub Philosopher

"I have made an important discovery . . . that alcohol, taken in sufficient quantities, produces all the effects of intoxication."
— Oscar Wilde, in conversation

The Whale's Pod

Bedwell Hotel and Marina
South Pender Island
Telephone: 629-3212

Hours: 11 a.m. - 1 a.m., Monday - Saturday; 11 a.m. - midnight, Sunday

The Navigator: From the ferry, follow the signs to Bedwell Harbour Road. The resort is on the south island, 18 kilometres from the ferry terminal.

There're not *too* many places on either of the Pender Islands to start a party, so if you're looking for a good time, do what many of the locals—and thousands of boaters—do and head towards **The Whale's Pod**. Bedwell Harbour Resort is one of the busiest destinations in all of the Gulf Islands: there are complete, recently renovated facilities for vacationers and moorage for 180 boats, while the presence of a Canada Customs office guarantees a huge traffic in pleasure craft either entering or returning to these southern B.C. waters. The Pod's beachside outdoor deck allows you to study all those sailboats and power yachts that are bobbing at the dock, while a gorgeous marine vista supplies an evocative backdrop.

Inside, the old-timey nautical photos make a nice contrast to the giant inflatable whale over the bar—and if you're there at one of those times when the staff are feeling frisky, the bartender might be mixing drinks with a waitress perched on his shoulder. The varnished pine floor looks good enough to dance on ... which is precisely why management chucked out the pool table to make space for the fleet-footed folk who crowd the place when the sun goes down and the music gets turned up.

Attractively tucked in at the base of a steep hill covered in fir and arbutus trees, Bedwell Harbour Resort offers cottages, condo-style rooms with balconies, a licensed dining room, gift shop, grocery store, laundromat, showers, heated pool, boat and bicycle rentals, boat charters and complete marine facilities. And as though that weren't

Gulf Islands_

enough, substantial improvements are already underway: big-money interests have just acquired the place, and a large hotel complex and a complement of upscale shops are expected to be finished by 1995.

Whether you've arrived by bicycle and just want to quaff a quick port-side pint, or have docked your sixty-foot yacht in anticipation of a long, libation-filled holdover, The Whale's Pod will extend a warm, West Coast welcome.

Beer Trivia

There was never more hypocrisy current in the United States than during Prohibition. In one droll instance, the jury hearing a bootlegging case itself became the subject of harsh legal scrutiny: it was accused of consuming all the evidence.

Molson Brewery, inaugurated in 1786, is North America's oldest continuously operated brewing company.

Sh-Qu-Ala

North Pender Island
Telephone: 629-3493

Hours: Noon - 1 a.m., Friday - Saturday; noon - 12:30 a.m., Sunday - Thursday

The Navigator: Located at Port Browning Marina. Turn left off Bedwell Harbour Road onto Hamilton Road, just past the gas station and store.

Sh-Qu-Ala is a romantic-sounding Indian word that translates into the more familiar "watering hole." But whichever language visitors choose, they'll certainly agree that it's an apt name for this attractive stone and wood pub, which is plunked down just above the beach at Port Browning Marina.

Where the Whale's Pod pub down-island at Bedwell Harbour has a tonier, yachtsman's atmosphere, Sh-Qu-Ala has a funky charm that seems more in tune with Gulf Island rhythms. Erected by the Henshaw family in the mid-1970s, this friendly pub was built around a West Coast Indian motif—appropriate enough, given that Sh-Qu-Ala sits on the site of an Indian fish camp dating from long ago. Heeding local legend that there was a curse on the land, the owners cleverly decided to install a totem pole in their longhouse-styled pub. Simon Charlie, a Quamichan carver, convinced the Henshaws that a grand "house pole" was needed. Chisels in hand, Simon produced an elegant, ten-foot totem that proudly dominates the pub. Its life-sized bear figure represents power (and in the bear's tummy is a mosquito in human form that will drive any evil spirits away).

When Simon delivered the house pole, he watched one of the pair of eagles that returns to the bay each summer as it fished in front of Sh-Qu-Ala. He was so struck by the bird's beauty and power that he went home and made the carving that now flies above the bar.

Friendly and folksy, the Sh-Qu-Ala has brought nothing but good luck to the innumerable tourists, boaters and locals wh have dropped in for the good times and good food in this particularly attractive marine setting. Whether you order a Caesar salad or a steak sandwich, a pint of ale or a wee dram of something more potent, the courteous service and relaxed atmosphere will persuade you that this is one "watering hole" that should never run dry.

Beer Trivia

Pilsner, the model for most Canadian beers, is a light and extremely refreshing beer with a striking hop character. Pilsener Urquell, which is brewed in Pilsen, Czechoslovakia, is the benchmark beer to which other Pilsners are compared.

Pub Philosopher

"There was a young fellow named Sydney
Who drank till he ruined a kidney,
It shrivelled and shrank
As he sat there and drank
But he had a good time at it, didn't he?"

The Hummingbird

Sturdies Bay Road, Galiano Island
Telephone: 539-5472

Hours: 11 a.m. - midnight, Sunday - Thursday; 11 a.m. - 1 a.m., Friday - Saturday

The Navigator: From the Sturdies Bay ferry terminal, head along the main road for one mile; the Hummingbird is on the right, just before the road diverges.

Started in 1984, the cedar-and-plaster **Hummingbird Pub** is like a country cottage. Sited at the edge of a cedar grove, this rustic, cabin-style building has wood floors, cosy seats and a convivial atmosphere: locals and tourists can mix in a relaxed manner, trading stories and maybe buying a round for a new group of friends. The Hummingbird also has an outdoor deck that is irresistible in summer. Complete with hanging flower baskets and the hummingbird feeders that attract this pub's tiny, whirring mascots, this funky patio may well convince ale-sipping travellers that they have found the secret to real happiness. And—at least in terms of Galiano—they'd be right, for this is the only pub on the island (and luckily it's a fine one!).

Ian, the present bartender, helped build the Hummingbird and he takes pride in ensuring that all the guests are treated well. The atmosphere is friendly and the food is particularly noteworthy. The five-page menu proudly trumpets that they are "purveyors of the finest pub food anywhere," and their Caesar salad and burger offer fairly convincing support for that claim.

The boating crowd is made particularly welcome at this landlocked pub: there's a special bus that runs between the marina and campgrounds near Montague and the Hummingbird; it's $2 for a return trip, with hourly departures between 5 and 11 p.m. This service is available from the May long weekend through to mid-September.

The present owners are Ron and Tracy Tekatch, who also run the Harbour House Hotel on Saltspring. Ron's been in the hospitality business for thirty years, and he ensures that his pub continues to please. Whether you drop in for some blues and jazz on a summer weekend, or need a lunchtime burger and a beer before getting your holiday properly underway, The Hummingbird will convince you that island living is a great way to go.

Beer Trivia

After Prohibition came into effect under the Volstead Act, thirsty Americans sought help from their compliant doctors. Legal prescriptions for "medicinal" liquor amounted to more than a million gallons per year.

The hop plant, a close relative of marijuana, contains a mild sedative called Lupulin. Highly hopped home brew has a more relaxing effect than the same quantity of commercial beer.

Bibliography

Berberoglu, H. *Brewing, Canadian Breweries and Home Brewing*. Toronto: Food and Beverage Consultants, 1987.

Berry, C.J.J. *Home Brewed Beers & Stouts*. Andover: Standard Press, 1984.

Butcher, Alan D. *Ale & Beer: A Curious History*. Toronto: McClelland and Stewart, 1989.

Kluckner, Michael. *Vanishing Victoria*. Vancouver: Whitecap Books, 1986.

McFarlan, Donald (ed.). *Guinness Book of World Records*. London: Guinness Publishing, 1991.

Mares, William. *Making Beer*. New York, Alfred A. Knopf, 1984.

Moore, William. *Home Beermaking*. Oakland: Ferment Press, 1980.

Ormsby, Margaret. *British Columbia: A History*. Toronto: Macmillan Company, 1971.

Reese, M.R. *Better Beer & How to Brew It*. Charlotte, Vermont: Garden Way Publishing, 1978.

Reksten, Terry. *"More English than the English"*. Victoria: Orca Book Publishers, 1986.

Reyd, Jane & Tyrrell, Bob. *The Pubs of B.C.* Victoria: Orca Book Publishers, 1988.

    Although Robert Moyes is rarely considered one of the city's most sober citizens, this Victoria native insists that his pubbing research was fueled by hot coffee rather than cold beer.

    Prior to his stint as a chronicler of the Island's best alehouses, he spent four hears before the masthead as the arts editor at *Monday Magazine*. A freelancer since 1989, Robert still contributes movie reviews to *Monday*. He published his first book, *Victoria: The Insider's Guide*, (Orca) in 1990.

    An ardent squash player, Robert is justly feared ... for the rather silly mesages on his answering machine that is, and not because of his squash strokes, which are as unconvincing as a B.C. politician's election promises. But whether he's just writing about beer or actually drinking the stuff, Robert is always ready to toast the high quality of pubbing on Vancouver Island.